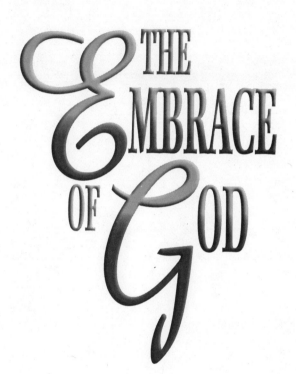

Dr. M. Lloyd Erickson

BETHANY HOUSE PUBLISHERS
MINNEAPOLIS, MINNESOTA 55438

Library of Congress Cataloging-in-Publication Data

CIP Data applied for

ISBN 1–55661–810–7   CIP

Why the M? Why M. Lloyd Erickson? I certainly don't want to appear stuffy or pompous or even academic. But I just couldn't write this book without the M. Here's why.

My father's name was Melvin Eddy Erickson. When I was born, my parents named me Melvin Lloyd Erickson. They never intended that my given name be Melvin—they always called me Lloyd. But initials were important back then, and they thought M.L. sounded better than L.M.

Although Dad has been gone for years now, I still think of him every day. I remember our talks while driving to school, our Ping-Pong tournaments, and our camping trips. More importantly, I remember him introducing me to our Heavenly Father.

That's why I couldn't possibly write a book about our heavenly Parent without the M.

I gratefully and lovingly dedicate these pages to the memory of the one who started my personal journey of knowing and loving Heavenly Father. Thanks, Dad.

DR. M. LLOYD ERICKSON is Director of the Counseling and Testing Center at Andrews University in Berrien Springs, Michigan. He maintains a limited private practice in Battle Creek, where he and his wife, Charlette, live. They have two adult children, Jonathan and Jennifer. Lloyd enjoys wilderness camping and canoeing—and talking about Heavenly Father's embraces.

Acknowledgments

Many wonderful friends played significant roles in the preparation of *Embrace*. I am especially indebted to:

Karen Mestemaker for delivering one of Heavenly Father's great hugs and increasing my awareness of His love for me.

Psychologists Dr. Nancy Zielke, Dr. Selma Chaij, and Nels Thompson; licensed professional counselor Dr. Margaret Dudley; pastors Ken Wilson, and Dale Leamon; and seminary professor Dr. Roger Dudley. You are extremely busy people and yet you eagerly took time to read and critique my manuscript. Your suggestions were invaluable. I am in your debt.

My colleagues at Andrews University's Counseling and Testing Center—Dr. Margaret Dudley, Dr. Don Wallace, Herdley Paolini, Dr. Penny Webster, and all our student interns. Also to Jane Morrison and our student secretary/receptionists. Our discussions following my *Embrace* devotionals were extremely helpful. And your encouragement kept me going.

Willis Callahan and the Camp Arrowhead committee.

Your invitation to speak at a weekend celebration in 1992 was the genesis of *Embrace*.

Andy Nash, my youthful "unofficial editor," for offering innumerable helpful suggestions. Monday nights will never be the same.

Charlotte, my wonderful wife, for being patient while I was preoccupied with the writing of *Embrace*. And for being my first and best critic as each chapter came "off the press." I am lucky to be sharing life with you.

Jonathan and Jennifer, my adult children, for "permitting" me to learn about fathering from our relationship. You have taught me much and I thank you for the privilege of being your Dad.

My treasured clients who teach me something new every day. I especially value what you have shown me about Heavenly Father. Incidentally, if you think you see yourself in *Embrace*—you don't. If you don't think you see yourself, well, it just could be . . .

Kevin Johnson and the BHP family for believing in the potential of this book. When other publishers refused to read unsolicited manuscripts, you took this one seriously. Thanks so much!

Heavenly Father for providing the inspiration for *Embrace*. In the process You often reminded me of a perfect illustration, clarified a confused thought, or supplied a meaningful phrase. I am grateful for the privilege of writing about You.

And to you, the reader, for playing an extremely important role—reading *Embrace*. I pray that this will be a significant experience in your life. Please accept *Embrace* as a hug from Heavenly Father. It's my honor to deliver it!

Contents

Abruptly Jesus broke into prayer: "Thank you, Father, Lord of heaven and earth. You've concealed your ways from sophisticates and know-it-alls, but spelled them out clearly to ordinary people. Yes, Father, that's the way you like to work."

Jesus resumed talking to the people, but now tenderly. "The Father has given me all these things to do and say. This is a unique Father-Son operation, coming out of Father and Son intimacies and knowledge. No one knows the Son the way the Father does, nor the Father the way the Son does. But I'm not keeping it to myself; I'm ready to go over it line by line with anyone willing to listen.

"Are you tired? Worn out? Burned out on religion? Come to me. Get away with me and you'll recover your life. I'll show you how to take a real rest. Walk with me and work with me—watch how I do it. Learn the unforced rhythms of grace. I won't lay anything heavy or ill-fitting on you. Keep company with me and you'll learn to live freely and lightly."

Matthew 11:25–30, The Message

INTRODUCTION

A Fresh Canvas

Father. What an emotion-packed word. For some people, just hearing or reading the term provokes terror. For others, anger. For still others, happiness or sadness or joy or love or anxiety. Similarly, the term *mother* elicits emotions lurking deep within us.

The reason *father* and *mother* prompt particular emotions is that we all have memories associated with the words. We are conscious of some of those memories. Other memories stir within the subconscious. Our histories, to a great extent, determine the feelings evoked by the words *father* and *mother.* And, as we shall see in the next chapter, they greatly impact our concept of our Heavenly Parent.

But what if we are wrong? What if our concepts of *father* and *mother* are based on limited or distorted information? More significantly, what if our view of Heavenly Father is a misperception?

Something happened last Christmas that reminded me of the pitfalls of making assumptions without appropriate investigation. In some situations, it can be dangerous to assume something too quickly. In others, it can be humorous.

For Christmas I had purchased my wife a small desktop radio/cassette player. Typical male gift, I guess. You know, practical. But it was something she wanted. Really! She wanted it to calm her work environment at the Kellogg Foundation. When Charlotte opened her brightly wrapped package she seemed pleased—if not surprised.

She kept the radio/cassette player on the kitchen counter for several days before taking it to her office. One morning while she was exercising, I thought I'd enjoy listening to her radio while I ate breakfast. This radio had lots of switches and gizmos. When I finally found the power button, some "music" erupted that would not have aided my digestive process. The dial said AM, so I decided to change to an FM station. But when I moved the switch it still said AM.

I thought I must have pushed the wrong button, so I rechecked. Yes, the setting was correct. I could get FM stations but the light still said AM. *Should say FM. Must be something wrong with the switch. I'll have to exchange the radio.*

After locating a listenable FM station, I settled into my cereal, toast, and orange juice. My breakfast was half eaten when I glanced at the radio and noticed the time. The *time.* The radio was also a clock. And then it hit me. If I sat there for a few more hours the AM would change to PM. It would never say *FM.* It was never intended to say FM.

Talk about feeling foolish. I'm certainly glad that I didn't pull that one in public. But it *was* funny. I had to tell my wife. And now I've shared it with you (you won't tell anyone will you?).

Preconceived ideas can be humorous. But they also can be dangerous.

Two thousand years ago God came to our world and few people recognized Him. The religious leaders said Jesus was an imposter because He didn't fit their expectations. God's church of that day was looking for a political leader to help them overthrow their foreign oppressors. They wanted temporal, not spiritual, blessings.

When Jesus didn't fit their preconceived idea of the Messiah, they rejected Him. When He talked of a kingdom of love and forgiveness, they mocked Him. When His message challenged their assumptions, they murdered Him.

I wonder: if God came in human form today, would we be any different than His people 2,000 years ago? Would we recognize Heavenly Father? Is it possible that we, too, have misperceptions regarding the type of person He is?

Our perceptions of Heavenly Father are largely based upon preconceived ideas developed through

the quality of our Sunday school training,

the classroom atmosphere during our early grades,

the type of sermons we have heard,

the nature of our spiritual conversations,

the scriptures we have read or not read, but mostly through the type of early parenting we experienced.

Thus, your personal profile of Heavenly Father may be of an angry person. Or a demanding, perfectionistic person. Or of an emotionally abusive, physically abusive, or sexually abusive person.

Your profile of Father may be of a distant, uncaring parent. Or a parent with so many interests He has no time for you.

Your profile may be that of a Father who has rejected or even abandoned you.

Or your profile may be that of an authority figure who rewards you when you do what is required.

But what if your perceptions are incorrect? What if you are like the church of old—thinking in terms of physical blessings while the real issues are spiritual? What if you are thinking in terms of radio frequency and you're actually dealing with time? What if you are viewing Heavenly Father through nearsighted eyes due to the "human-ness" of your parents? What if no one has ever told you the truth about Heavenly Father?

In the past few years I have been challenging some of my long-held, preconceived ideas. Especially about God the Father. This process has resulted in a rich spiritual journey, a deepening personal relationship with my Heavenly Father. I hope that as you read this book the Holy Spirit will impress you also to take a fresh look at your Heavenly Father.

Try to look at Him with an open mind.

Try to view Him without any preconceived notions.

Try to set aside your baggage.

Try to see Him again for the first time.

I promise you it will be worth the effort. Whatever has been your lifelong personal profile of your Heavenly Father, I invite you now to

grab your paintbrushes,

rinse off the thickened old paint,

set up a new canvas,

seek renewed inspiration,

dip a brush into a fresh color on the palette of God's Word, and begin painting a fresh, clear, accurate profile of Heavenly Father.

Enjoy the process. And enjoy the emerging beauty of His profile.

For all who are led by the Spirit of God are sons [and daughters] of God.

And so we should not be like cringing, fearful slaves, but we should behave like God's very own children, adopted into the bosom of his family, and calling to him, "Father, Father."

For his Holy Spirit speaks to us deep in our hearts, and tells us that we really are God's children.

Romans 8:14–16, TLB (bracketed mine)

ONE

Early Tracings of Heavenly Father

When artists prepare to draw a subject's face, they often begin with "construction lines." These lines consist of an oval the approximate size of the face they intend to sketch and a large cross (+) placed over the oval.

Construction lines are functional and foundational. They're not pretty. They don't resemble the face of any model. But they are necessary in order to obtain proper proportions.

This chapter contains the construction lines for our profile of Heavenly Father. These beginning marks will not be pretty as a completed portrait, but they are important. They establish the foundation for the concepts that follow.

Where do we get our initial perception of God? Research indicates that our view of Heavenly Father is conceived long before we have the ability to comprehend the idea of an unseen God. As we began establishing our initial relationships with our parents, we started forming "deep patterns of understanding."[1] These earliest perceptions of our parents provided the early tracings of our profile of Heavenly Father.

Many research studies have demonstrated the relationship between our early perceptions of parents and our adult concepts of Heavenly Father.[2] One study found that our image of God is related to our image of *ideal* parents as well as our actual parents.[3]

Other studies suggest that a child's concept of God is derived from both mother and father.[4] Thus we may grow up seeing God as having both paternal and maternal characteristics.

Angry, loving, violent, punitive, uninvolved, judgmental, or caring images of Heavenly Father are closely related to parental characteristics. We carry these perceptions with us into adulthood. J. B. Phillips calls this influence a "parental hangover."[5]

It's as though we were born in a house that had only one window. From that window we viewed the significant people and events in our early lives. One day (or perhaps many days) stones were thrown at our window. The stones may have been pebbles of imperfect parenting or rocks of abuse. The extent of the damage depends upon the intensity and duration of these early experiences. But to a lesser or greater degree our windowpanes have been cracked and our vision distorted. We have developed misperceptions of Heavenly Father.[6]

These early misconceptions intensified when we learned that Jesus told us to call God "Our Father in heaven" (Matthew 6:9, NIV). And later in life we may have discovered that Scripture from beginning to end speaks of God as Father. In Moses' recitation of song before the assembled Israelites he said, "Is this the way you repay the Lord, O foolish and unwise people? Is he not your Father, your Creator, who made you and formed you?" (Deuteronomy 32:6, NIV).

Indeed, many times in the Old Testament God is referred to as Father.[7] But it wasn't until Jesus elaborated on the subject of Father that a clearer profile began to emerge.[8] He indicated that His Father is also our Father. He told Mary Magdalene, "Do not hold on to me, for I have not yet returned to the Father. Go instead to my brothers [His followers] and tell them, 'I am returning to my Father and your Father, to my God and your God' " (John 20:17, NIV, bracketed mine). And the depiction of God's Fatherhood continues throughout the New Testament, ending in the book of Revelation.[9]

So the terminology of Scripture reinforces our youthful deduction that God is like our parents.

The problem is that we all had imperfect parents. Our perception of Heavenly Father, then, needs at least some correction. But these early images are extremely difficult to change. Just when we think we've developed a new perspective, we slip back into responding to Heavenly Father on the basis of our early distorted images.[10]

To change those misperceptions takes effort—ongoing effort. You're already doing some of that by thinking through the concepts I am presenting here. But your work will need to continue beyond the final page of this book.

In order to get this process started you must be willing to reexamine your perception of Heavenly Father. Without a conscious effort on your part you will maintain the perceptions your parents unwittingly gave you. And that would be tragic because the devil has distorted parenthood just as he has distorted everything else in the world. Jesus said that the devil is "a murderer from the beginning, not holding to the truth, for there is no truth in him. When he lies, he speaks his native language, for he is a liar and the father of lies" (John 8:44, NIV).

The last thing the devil wants is for us to understand the truth about Heavenly Father. He communicates his distortions to us not only through our families of origin, but through the world around us.

As adults, if we were to believe everything we hear, we would perceive Heavenly Father as being the cause of disease, famine, storms, death. God certainly gets a lot of bad press.

Insurance companies refer to catastrophes as "acts of God." Some Christians blame God when tragedy occurs in their lives. Others perpetuate a picture of a Heavenly Father who is far removed from the daily experiences of His children. Probably even *we* have at times forgotten the type of wonderful Heavenly Father we have. In our anguish we may have blamed God for physical pain, for problems in our lives, or for the death of someone we dearly love.

I've done it. You've done it. Even Martha did it. And so did her sister Mary. Their brother Lazarus had become gravely ill and the sisters sent word to Jesus. They had witnessed Jesus heal the sick and they knew He would want to restore health to his friend Lazarus. But Jesus delayed two days before even starting His journey to their home in Bethany. By the time He arrived Lazarus had been buried four days.

Martha met Jesus with these words, "Lord, if you had been here, my brother would not have died" (John 11:21, NIV). When Mary came to Jesus, she made a similar statement (v. 32). Their initial words sound a lot like, *Where were you when I really needed you? Don't you care enough to be here in my time of need? Don't your friends matter to you?*

As Jesus observed the intense grief of Mary and Martha, He was deeply moved. He wept. He didn't just have watery eyes. The original language of the Gospel of John indicates that He sobbed convulsively.

Why did Jesus experience such deep emotion? Observers at the scene said it was because of how deeply Jesus loved Lazarus (v. 36). But that's an unlikely reason because Jesus knew He would raise Lazarus to life in just a few minutes.

Others have said that Jesus was empathizing with Martha and Mary. I'm sure there's truth in that observation.

But I believe the most basic reason for the intensity of Jesus' feelings was that even His friends didn't fully recognize who He was. They didn't comprehend that He was "the resurrection and the life" (v. 25). He grieved because after all the time He had spent with them, they still didn't understand His character. They still didn't really know Him. They still didn't trust Him.

I believe Heavenly Father also grieves. He grieves today when we have an inaccurate profile of Him due to experiences with our own parents. He grieves when we fail to mature in our perception of Him. He grieves when we believe the devil's lies about the kind of Person He is.

It seems that the devil's lies about Heavenly Father are everywhere. They crept into His early church. And they still find their way into Christian circles.

There are many reasons why it's important to have an accurate, clear profile of Heavenly Father. First, He *wants* us to know the truth about himself. He has nothing to hide.[11]

Second, it's crucial to us and our salvation that we know Him.[12]

For . . .

As we envision an accurate profile of Heavenly Father, we begin to truly appreciate His gift of salvation.

As we experience how much Heavenly Father loves us, we are freed to return His love and to share it with His other children.

As we are humbled by His indescribable love, we begin to realize our unworthiness.

As we feel secure in His care, we sense our value.

As we understand the truth about Heavenly Father, we trust Him even though we cannot fully comprehend Him.

Only by getting to know our Heavenly Father can we obtain optimal spiritual and emotional health.

Christians are fond of the term "good news" (gospel). Usually we think of the good news as being the news about Jesus' life, death, and resurrection and the truth that we can live forever in God's presence.

But the "good news" doesn't stop there. After all, what would it be like to spend eternity with an angry God? Or a perfectionistic God? Or an emotionally withdrawn God? The *great* news is the type of individual our Heavenly Father actually is.

Could you use some great news? If so, keep reading. There's plenty of it in the following chapters.

But first I must warn you that the process of painting a fresh profile of Heavenly Father can be painful. Isn't that ironic? Good news associated with pain? But this pain has nothing to do with who Heavenly Father is.

The concepts I present may trigger painful memories. You may have had a childhood where your parents were hurtful. It doesn't matter if you're eight or eighty—what you experienced still hurts a great deal. Perhaps for years you have desperately attempted not to think about it.

The problem with this approach is that your emotional and spiritual growth gets stuck.

Rather than denying these hurts and fears, make time to face them. I believe one of the best ways to do this is with someone (perhaps a Christian therapist) who can help you form a more accurate picture of good parenting. One purpose of *The Embrace of God* is to help you in that process.

Sketching a profile of Heavenly Father may also be painful for parents distressed over children who have made harmful choices. You may be blaming yourself for your children's waywardness.

Please be assured that my purpose is not to heap blame or induce pain or guilt. There's probably plenty of that already. Instead, I hope to encourage spiritual and emotional growth by pointing you to the One who can heal your pain and release your guilt.

Rather than focusing on ourselves, let's look at Heavenly Father. As we behold the beauty of His character, we will be changed into His likeness.

The process of sketching Heavenly Father won't end with reading *Embrace*. It won't even end in this lifetime. There will be more to learn of Him throughout eternity.

Still, we must start painting an *accurate* profile. Although what we currently can see is only "a poor reflection as in a mirror,"[13] let's come to the canvas. Although we may be only novice artists, let's pick up clean brushes.

There are many features of Heavenly Father's profile that we *can* clearly see. There's much about Him that we *can* comprehend. Let's sketch carefully and accurately.

Our "construction lines" are in place.

Let's begin.

Notes

1. Bruce Narramore, *Parenting With Love and Limits* (Grand Rapids: Zondervan Publishing House, 1987), p. 85.
2. The best literature review I have discovered is: Kenneth E. Hyde, *Religion in Childhood and Adolescence: A Comprehensive Review of the Research* (Birmingham, Ala.: Religious Education Press, 1990).
3. Hyde, p. 65.
4. A. Godin and M. Hallez, "Parental Images and Divine Paternity," *From Religious Experience to Religious Attitude* (Brussels: Lumen Vitae, 1964, and Chicago: Loyola University Press, 1965). Mark Keyser and Gary Collins, "Parental Image and the Concept of God: An Evangelical Protestant-Catholic Comparison," *Journal of Psychology and Theology*, 2, no. 1, pp. 69–80.
5. J. B. Phillips, *Your God Is Too Small* (New York: Macmillan Company, 1970), pp. 19–20.
6. With appreciation to Patsy Clairmont, *Under His Wings* (Carmel, New York: Guideposts, 1994), pp. 73–77.
7. See Psalm 89:26; 103:13; Isaiah 63:16; 64:8.
8. See John 5:16–30; 6:44–46; 8:16–30; 10:15–18; 14:2, 6–31.
9. See Revelation 1:6; 2:27; 3:5,21; 14:1.
10. Narramore, p. 87.
11. See John 14:5–14.
12. See John 17:3.
13. See 1 Corinthians 13:12, NIV.

*I have spoken of these matters very guardedly, but the time will come when this will not be necessary and I will tell you plainly all about the Father. Then you will present your petitions over my signature! And I won't need to ask the Father to grant you these requests, for **the Father himself loves you dearly** because you love me and believe that I came from the Father. Yes, I came from the Father into the world and will leave the world and return to the Father.*

John 16:25–28, TLB (emphasis mine)

TWO

Never Too Busy for You

Omnipresence. You've probably heard the word. You might even know what it means. It's a term theologians use to describe God's ability to be "present everywhere simultaneously."[1]

But what does that mean in practical terms? How does that concept impact *your* daily life? In the next few chapters we will profile this distinctive trait of Heavenly Father.

Please remember: *Embrace* is not a critique of human parenting. We readily acknowledge that we are all imperfect parents. Rather than inducing guilt, I hope to encourage greater understanding of the beauty of God's character and to promote spiritual growth.

As we walk together through this book, I need you to know something. I will be sharing many experiences from my work as a clinical psychologist. Be assured that I value my clients far too much to compromise their privacy. Besides, I could never break confidentiality. But these good people have taught me so much about Heavenly Father. I need to share it with you. So I've changed the names and nonessential details. What you will read is the essence of what I have learned from their stories.

Let's take a look at the father who is too busy. (We could use the term *mother*, but I will use *father* since that's the model Jesus used.)

Too busy. This father may even be home much of the time. But he is wrapped up in his own interests and pursuits. He's

paying the bills,
adding a room on the house,
bowling in the league,
drinking with the guys,
browsing the Internet,
working overtime at the plant,
completing a job at the office, or even
doing the work of the church.

You know the scene. Probably all too well! This father just doesn't make time to truly give of himself to his sons and daughters.

Recently the Smith family came to my office for an assessment of their problems. The parents had recently married. Both brought to this relationship children from previous marriages. This was a family in need of blending.

The identified patient was the fourteen-year-old son of Mr. Smith. Rob was acting out his frustrations. Mr. Smith made it clear that he wanted to solve the problem with medication. You, too, have probably dreamed of a magic pill that would make your children behave!

As the assessment concluded, I told Mr. Smith in private that, in my professional opinion, medication was not the answer. I recommended that Mr. Smith spend some special time with Rob. Rob seemed to need his father—especially at this time. He needed to be assured that his father was still there for him. And I recommended that the entire family become involved in family therapy.

But Mr. Smith insisted on medication. I arranged for a consultation with the psychiatrist on our team. She agreed that medication would be an inappropriate treatment. So the family did begin therapy. Unfortunately, Mr. Smith seldom came. He was busy

playing golf with his friends,
showing off his new Corvette,
visiting with his buddies, or
any of a dozen other activities.

This, I learned, was typical of Mr. Smith. He was seldom at home either. This left the new Mrs. Smith caring for her children *and* his children. That didn't make her very happy. It was putting a great strain on the marriage.

Unfortunately, Mr. Smith continued to be too busy for his family. His most recent tactic was attempting to find a residential treatment center for Rob. He thought if he could get Rob out of the house—get rid of Rob—his problems would be over. All of this in spite of the recommendations of two doctors who clearly told Mr. Smith that what Rob needed was his father. Rob needed to feel loved. With all the recent changes, Rob needed the assurance that he was still important to his father. The prognosis for this family is fair at best, because Mr. Smith continues to be too busy for his children.

Were your parents ever too busy for you? Were there times when you really needed them and they weren't there for you? Jesus understands that situation. On at least one occasion even Joseph and Mary were preoccupied parents.

You will remember the story. At age twelve, Jesus made the annual trip to Jerusalem with his parents. As the Passover feast progressed, Mary and Joseph got caught up in the festivities. They worshiped at the temple. They socialized with old friends. They ate delicious food. They visited with family they hadn't seen for a year. They enjoyed the break from their hard work in Nazareth. But eventually the celebrating came to an end. The couple started the journey home.

But there was a problem. In their busyness they forgot Jesus. A day's journey toward Nazareth and they realized that Jesus wasn't in their traveling party. Can you imagine their desperate thoughts as they retraced their dusty steps?

What have we done? We were so busy that we lost our son. No, we've lost God's Son. We've lost the Messiah!

For three days they were separated from Jesus. Like most parents, Mary and Joseph were relieved to find their son. And, like most parents, they blamed their son for getting lost. "His mother said to him, 'Son, why have you treated us like this? Your father and I have been anxiously searching for you'" (Luke 2:48, NIV).

Yes, Jesus understands what it is like to have preoccupied parents.

Have you ever thought that your *Heavenly* Father is too busy for you? Be honest. Has that thought ever troubled you?

He's "Chairman of the Board." He has a lot to do up there. There are a million and one things calling for His attention. He has an entire universe to run. He has a million prayers to answer. And many people have more painful problems than I do. Think of the most recent earthquake victims, the latest war refugees, and people without shelter and food.

Listen, friend, to this precious truth. The relationship between you and your Heavenly Father is unique. It's as though there were not another person on the earth. It's as though there were not another soul in the universe. Because He is who He is, you don't have to share His attention with anyone. You are His special child. That's one of the benefits of having an omnipresent Father.

"This is the confidence we have in approaching God: that if we ask anything according to his will, he hears us. And if we know that he hears us—whatever we ask—we know that we have what we asked of him" (1 John 5:14–15, NIV).

Is your Heavenly Father too busy for you? No way. Not a chance. You may be too busy for Him, but your Heavenly Father is *never* too busy for you. Look at what your Father tells you through His Son. "Lo, I am with you *alway*, even unto the end of the world" (Matthew 28:20, KJV).

Is the world still here? If you are reading this, we can assume that it is. Then your Heavenly Father is still with you.

Years ago I knew a pastor in Canada named Lawton Lowe. He loved this passage. He thought it was written especially for him. The King James Version you just read says, "Lo, I am with you." Lawton's spelling wasn't terrific. He thought it said, "Lowe, I am with you." Isn't that beautiful? A personal promise of God's presence.

Taking the cue from Pastor Lowe, I can hear my Heavenly Father saying, "Lloyd, I am with you always." Or, "Lloyd, I am *always* with you."

Why don't you try it? Put your name in the verse. It could sound strange at first. But I think you'll grow to like it. Go ahead. The message is intended for you. Just as it was intended for Jesus' first followers. So say it. Claim it. Believe it.

"(Your name), I am with you. I am with you *always*. I am *always* with you. I am with you even to the end of the world. Amen." Amen!

You have a Father who is *never* too busy for you. He will *always* be with you. He just told you so—personally!

Notes

1. *The American Heritage College Dictionary*, third edition (Boston: Houghton Mifflin Company, 1993).

When he was still a long way off, his father saw him. His heart pounding, he ran out, embraced him, and kissed him. The son started his speech; "Father, I've sinned against God, I've sinned before you; I don't deserve to be called your son ever again."

But the father wasn't listening. He was calling to the servants, "Quick. Bring a clean set of clothes and dress him. Put the family ring on his finger and sandals on his feet. Then get a grain-fed heifer and roast it. We're going to feast! We're going to have a wonderful time! My son is here—given up for dead and now alive! Given up for lost and now found!" And they began to have a wonderful time.

Luke 15:20–24, The Message

THREE

Glimpses of a Father Who Hugs

His son was missing. But there were no missing person posters. No all-points bulletins. And no search parties. The reason? The son hadn't been mugged. He hadn't been kidnapped. There was no ransom note. This son left because he wanted to leave.

You know the story. We usually call it "the story of the prodigal son." I think a more appropriate title is "the story of the loving father." See if you agree.

Sonny gets bored living at home and heads for the attractions of the big city. His father misses him tremendously. Every day he leaves the house and walks to their property line. Shielding his eyes from the bright Mediterranean sun, he squints at the horizon. Every day he comes. Every day he looks. And every day he trudges slowly home with tears trickling down his aging cheeks.

One day, as usual, Father treks to his well-worn observation post. His eyesight has grown hazy. But he goes to look anyway. He looks . . . and looks. . . . He imagines movement on the horizon. He watches intently. He *does* see movement. Someone is coming. And there's something familiar about that walk. Then he knows! He runs and stumbles as fast as his old legs will take him to greet his son.

Tell me, what does this father say to his son?

Now, just where have you been all this time? Where is all the money you took with you? You look like you just came out of a pig pen!

He says none of those things. Instead he runs to his son, throws his arms around him, gives him a huge hug, and kisses him. Then he throws a welcome home party.[1]

What a beautiful sketch of an emotionally involved parent.

But not all parents are like that. Perhaps you grew up with an emotionally absent parent. Your mother may have been emotionally withdrawn. Or your father might have kept aloof and uninvolved. If so, it would be natural to assume that your Heavenly Father is also emotionally absent. There is good news for you.

Several years ago I was involved in psychotherapy with a family. As the McGees became more comfortable in that therapeutic environment, they began to be less cautious. They really started working on problem areas. This takes much courage.

Mr. McGee demonstrated a willingness to be vulnerable when he confessed that he never told anyone in his family that he loved them. I decided to push him a bit further. "Mr. McGee," I questioned, "if you don't tell Ann and the children that you love them, how *can* they tell that you love them?" I thought he would say something like, "I go to work and bring them home a paycheck," or, "I keep the yard nice." But he was much too honest for that. There was a pregnant silence. Finally, through watering eyes, he said, "I guess they really couldn't tell."

At a previous session it was Mrs. McGee who stated that she sometimes went to the store just to hear a kind word. "Thanks for shopping at K-Mart!" *Thanks for shopping at K-Mart*—the kindest words in Ann's day! How tragic. Fortunately, this father's confession marked the beginning of significant changes in the McGee family.

Our profile of Heavenly Father demonstrates that He is not emotionally absent. This, indeed, is wonderful news. Peter put it this way: "Cast all your anxiety on him because he cares for you" (1 Peter 5:7, NIV).

Your Father invites you to share your joys, your fears, your sorrows, and your needs with Him. He will never tire of carrying your load. He will never grow weary in listening to your voice. No sincere prayer can exist in your mind without His taking an *immediate* interest.

It sounds good, doesn't it? Almost too good to be true. It may contrast sharply with the experience you've had with your father. Perhaps you can relate more easily to Kathy's experience. Kathy was in therapy when she wrote the following letter, an elegant portrayal of the intense pain of growing up with an emotionally withdrawn father.

> Dear Dad,
>
> For some time now I've been seeing a psychologist. In the course of my therapy, I've come to understand how much my childhood has affected me. To help me deal with that, I'm writing you this letter.
>
> As an adult, I can now better understand that your life wasn't easy. What I don't understand is your treatment of me. My earliest memory of you (and I have no idea how old I was but I'm guessing three or four) was one day when you came home from work and Mom said, "Your father's home," and I ran and hid. I don't know why I was afraid of you. It's really the only memory I have of you during my earliest years.

Later I remember the fights between you and Mom—loud, screaming arguments. I remember being terrified. One time you made Donna and me sit on the couch while the two of you went at it. You wanted us to hear what you had to say. I don't remember what you said. But I vividly remember how frightened I was.

But the biggest hurt of all was your indifference toward me. Other than the perfunctory good-night kiss, I don't remember you ever holding me, hugging me—even putting your arm around me, or telling me that you loved me. Do you have any idea how difficult that was for a little girl—or a grown woman?

When I was eleven or twelve, Uncle Willie came up to me and put his arm around me. It was the first time I remember being hugged—at least by a man. It was such a memorable event that I wrote it in my diary. I hadn't realized how starved I was for affection.

I was never able to express my feelings, because I never learned how. Not only was expressing my feelings not encouraged, it was forbidden. When I was ten or eleven, you saw me crying and told me you never wanted to see me cry again. I was very hurt and angry with you. I determined that not only you, but nobody would ever see me cry—would ever know that I was hurt.

Now I'm paying the price. Now I'm crying for all the times I couldn't cry before.

Just before you died, you visited me. I remember sitting at the dining room table and you came up behind me and put your hand on my shoulder. I was thirty-six years old, and it was the first time I had experienced any display of affection from you. One month later, you died.

I cried at your funeral, but not because I missed you. I cried because I didn't miss you. Your death left no void in my life, no ache in my heart. Instead, the ache was because of what we never had.

As I write this now, I can hardly see the page because of my tears. I never sat in your lap, never was cuddled in your arms, never was told how special I was or that I was loved or cherished, and I never was able to talk to you about my problems.

I don't hate you for this; I'm not even angry with you. I'm sad for you—and for me. I'm sorry for a man whose death made no difference in his daughter's life.

I couldn't say all these things to you if you were alive, because I wouldn't want to hurt you. But this is supposed to make me feel better. We'll see. . . .

I'm not sure if I loved you—I tried.

Now I'm left to deal with feelings that I don't understand and can't express. I'm glad you're at peace. I wish I were.

Love, Kathy

I am grateful for Kathy's willingness to share her deep feelings with you. You may have suffered similar pain, and it helps to know that you're not alone. Let's thank Heavenly Father that He is not a Parent who withdraws His love and affection from His children.

Recently I was introduced to an unfamiliar verse of Scripture through Max Lucado's book *When God Whispers Your Name*. I will be forever grateful to Max for his inspiring books. I am especially thankful for learning about Psalm 56:8.

David is talking to God. He says, "You have seen me tossing and turning through the night." Incredible. As I restlessly tossed and turned last night, wondering how I could best convey these thoughts to you, He was observing. He was concerned. My Father was there for me.

The Psalmist continues, "You [Heavenly Father] have collected all my tears and preserved them in your bottle! You have recorded every one in your book" (Psalm 56:8, TLB, bracketed mine).

Amazing, isn't it? Your Heavenly Father collects *your* tears. An emotionally uninvolved Father? No way!

This verse of Scripture was so exciting that I immediately shared it with several colleagues. They, too, were blessed. Dr. Peggy Dudley said, "You know, I heard somewhere that there actually were tear bottles back in Bible times."

So I telephoned the Horn Archaeological Museum. The archaeologist informed me that many tear bottles had been uncovered while excavating ancient tombs. Scholars believe that loved ones and other mourners collected their tears in these small bottles. Then they buried the bottled tears with the loved one. They wanted everyone to realize how much the deceased person was missed and loved. So David was using a familiar custom to describe God's tender care for His children.

I went to the museum and found the archaeologists to be extremely kind and trusting. They loaned me a genuine tear bottle for a weekend. It was more than 2,000 years old. What an honor it was to share this verse and display the tear bottle to a congregation of worshipers. (More on that story in the next chapter.)

In your profile of Heavenly Father, can you visualize Him collecting *your* tears in such a bottle? It's probably difficult to imagine. But Scripture says it's true! Your Father certainly must care about your worries, your pain, and your sorrows. And if that isn't enough, He records them all in a book. He certainly sounds like an emotionally involved Father.

Some years ago I experienced a terribly low point in my life. Normally I take things pretty much in stride. But several painful situations were occurring. I became extremely discouraged.

One night in desperation I prayed, "Dear Father, I need to know you're with me. I need to know you care." Then I added impulsively, "Father, please give me a hug!" My words startled me. I had never heard a prayer like that.

God hugging me? The God of heaven reaching out and warmly embracing me?

I pondered the request.

A hug would feel awfully good right now.

I decided to watch for Heavenly Father's hug. And I continued to pray for one.

The next day I went to a shop to pick up my lawn tractor. It had been there for repair several times in the previous few weeks. And they had charged for *not* fixing it. I fully expected to be charged for the most recent work. I came prepared to vent my frustrations.

Surprise! The gentleman smiled. The tractor was ready and there was no additional charge.

A mile or two down the highway, reality finally hit me. I'm a little slow catching on sometimes. I shouted to no one in particular, "I'VE JUST BEEN HUGGED!" Tears trickled down my cheeks. It felt so good to feel the touch, the strong embrace, the enfolding grasp of my Heavenly Father.

That could have been the end of the story. But it wasn't. Not many hours went by before I found myself praying, "Father, that hug was so nice. I appreciate it so very much. But you know, I've been feeling so terrible. I need another hug. This time, could you make it a really, really big hug?"

Kind of childlike, don't you think? I thought so, too. I still think so. But I am comforted by Jesus' words, "I tell you the truth, unless you change and become like little children, you will never enter the kingdom of heaven. Therefore, whoever humbles himself like this child is the greatest in the kingdom of heaven" (Matthew 18:3–4, NIV).

Later that week Marty arrived at my office for her weekly session. Marty was a junior high school teacher. We had been working together for a year and she had made tremendous progress. Today she was bubbling with happiness.

Marty related that she had been walking toward her school's year-end assembly when someone delayed her for a few minutes. They walked together into the auditorium, a few minutes late. Someone took Marty's elbow and escorted her through the audience to the platform. Marty was stunned.

The superintendent of education was making announcements. Marty was so nervous that she didn't comprehend what he was saying. She noticed her husband come in the back door. *What's he doing here?* He came to the platform and stood beside her. Then she heard the superintendent introduce her two young daughters, who joined them on the platform. And then her mother appeared. *Mother lives two hours from here.*

There was a dramatic pause. The attention of the students was riveted on the scene. Then the announcement—Marty had been chosen as the school district's first Teacher of the Year! There was wild applause as she was presented with an engraved plaque. Then one of her students sang a musical tribute.

Tears stream down Marty's face as she shares her story with me. My eyes water, too, as I am deeply moved by her emotions. From her handbag, Marty carefully pulls out the plaque. It was a wonderful tribute to her. But I was not prepared for what happened next.

Marty looked up at me through tear-filled eyes. "Dr. E, as my student was singing, the tears just rolled down my face. I looked at all the special people who had been called to share this moment with me. And I had this thought. Everyone important in my life was here—except one. I wished *you* could have been there! You have had such a big part in helping me become who I am."

Instantly I knew! My Heavenly Father had reached down and wrapped His strong arms around me. He had given me a very special hug. Tears flowed down my cheeks, too.

One of the areas we had worked on in therapy was Marty's spiritual life. So I had the wonderful opportunity to share with her how she had just permitted God to use her to deliver His loving embrace.

Your Heavenly Father has warm hugs for you, too.

Do you remember the story of the loving father at the beginning of the chapter? Jesus told it first to His followers. He wanted them to know that His Father loves to hug His children. I believe Heavenly Father *still* enjoys hugging His people. Little hugs. Huge hugs. He enjoys them all. He enjoys hugging you, too.

Heavenly Father is never too busy to be interested in you. And He isn't an emotionally distant parent. He loves to put His arms around you. In this context, consider this familiar passage of Scripture.

"Jerusalem! Jerusalem!" (you could insert the name of your city here). ". . . How often I've ached to embrace your children, the way a hen gathers her chicks under her wings" (Matthew 23:37, Message).

Without doing damage to the intent of the verse, you could also read it, "(Your first name)! How often I've ached to embrace you, the way a hen gathers her chicks under her wings." What a thrill! God wants to hug *you*!

But sadly the verse concludes, "And you wouldn't let me."

Friend, Heavenly Father longs to hold you in His arms. He has special hugs for you. But you must let Him. If someone is emotionally withdrawn in your spiritual relationship, it is *not* your Heavenly Father. You know who that leaves!

What do you say? Let's permit Heavenly Father to give us *all* the hugs that He so much wants us to experience.

Notes

1. See Luke 15:11–24.

Which of you, if his son asks for bread, will give him a stone? Or if he asks for a fish, will give him a snake? If you, then, though you are evil, know how to give good gifts to your children, how much more will your Father in heaven give good gifts to those who ask him!

Matthew 7:9–11, NIV

FOUR

Hugs, Hugs, and More Hugs

Good parents love their children. They are affectionate with them. They enjoy giving to their sons and daughters. Good parents rejoice in their children's happiness. They are pleased with their children's thankfulness.

Human parenting at its best is a reasonably accurate profile of Heavenly Father. Perhaps that's why He chose the family model to tell us about himself. And to explain the type of relationship He wants with us.[1]

But Heavenly Father's motives are purer. His hugs are more desperately needed. His love is stronger and deeper. And He finds innumerable ways to express His love to us. Heavenly Father is a real hugger. He hugs us hundreds of times each day. Unfortunately, we are not conscious of many of them. Often we take His hugs for granted. We grow to expect them. We think we're entitled to them. And we become oblivious to the meaning behind His embraces.

Let's change that pattern. Let's be grateful children. Let's begin right now by recognizing the types of hugs He so lovingly gives us.

His Practical Hugs

Some of God's most profound hugs are experienced in the simple everyday things of life. (Actually, there is nothing simple about them.) Think about the hug involved

in the gift of a glass of clear, pure water,
in a breath of fresh, sweet air,
in a good night's sleep,
in standing on solid ground,
in having food on the table,
in having some measure of health.

We take so much for granted. Until the water is polluted. Until our lungs struggle for air. Until we haven't slept for weeks. Until we survive an earthquake. Until money or food is in short supply. Until our health is depleted.

When we take time to consider them, we realize these are vitally important hugs. Let's appreciate them *now*. Let's not wait *until*. We may not be rich in the things of this world. But God has met our basic needs—and more. These hugs demonstrate His love and concern for us.

His Aesthetic Hugs

Heavenly Father's hugs go far beyond providing for our basic needs. He throws in color, texture, flavor, fragrance, touch, music. . . . If the hugs just discussed are practical hugs, these are aesthetic hugs.

God's love for you and me is expressed through beauty. He made this world beautiful. And He created it for our enjoyment.

In your imagination, would you be willing to take a

brief walk with me? Let's walk down a seldom-used dirt "road" that wanders through the woods behind my house. The birds are singing their spring songs. Chickadees, sparrows, warblers, goldfinches, woodpeckers, bluebirds, and other songsters produce a wonderfully natural choir. We feel like joining the chorus of "How Great Thou Art."

High overhead we hear the honking Canada geese winging their way northward. Our ears catch a drumming sound. A ruffed grouse is in his mating ritual. Observing God's feathered creatures brings to mind some words of Jesus. "Two sparrows are sold for a farthing, aren't they? Yet not a single sparrow falls to the ground without your father's knowledge. The very hairs of your head are all numbered. Never be afraid then—you are far more valuable than sparrows" (Matthew 10:29–31, Phillips). And we know we have been hugged by our Father.

As we walk, we come upon an ugly scene. A long-abandoned school bus. A rejected relic of a dumptruck. Other junk. These scars to the landscape remind us of the blight of sin in our world. This is definitely not God's work. It's the devil who works to degrade the beautiful. We remember Jesus' parable of the farmer who sowed good seed in his field. But while his crew slept, an enemy came and sowed weeds in his wheatfield. Jesus clearly stated that enemy is the devil.[2] We hurry past these ugly reminders of sin. And again we slow our pace to enjoy Heavenly Father's embraces.

The birch, hickory, and maple trees are turning green. White blossomed dogwoods beautify the woodlands. Pushing through the forest floor, a variety of wild flowers respond to the warming season. And we remember Jesus' words, "Consider how the lilies grow. They do not labor or spin. Yet I tell you, not even Solomon in all his splendor was dressed like one of these. If that is how God clothes the grass of the field, which is here today, and tomorrow is thrown into the fire, how much more will he clothe you,

O you of little faith!" (Luke 12:27–28, NIV). And we feel very special.

We leave the woods and enter a hayfield. From the top of a hill we catch fox kits playing at the mouth of their den. In the evening light we watch the kits frolic. And we remember that Jesus said, "Foxes have holes and birds of the air have nests, but the Son of Man has no place to lay his head" (Matthew 8:20, NIV). And we feel thankful for heaven's best Gift.

As the shadows lengthen, six or seven whitetail deer amble into the field to graze. Suddenly their heads jerk upward. Their faces and ears point toward us. They watch us curiously. We don't move—and they relax. As we watch, our minds recall words from the psalmist. "As the deer pants for streams of water, so my soul pants for you, O God. My soul thirsts for God, for the living God" (Psalm 42:1–2, NIV). Indeed! That's why we're out on this walk together.

As the sun sets, we enjoy the multicolors reflecting on distant clouds. And we remember what we have seen and heard and felt. "God is love" (1 John 4:8, NIV) was proclaimed by everything we have experienced. We have, indeed, experienced many Fatherly hugs.

The fresh wild violets smiled, *Your Heavenly Father loves you.*

The bluebirds sang, *Your Father cares.*

The breeze on the quivering new leaves whispered, *Your Father is with you even when He seems silent.*

Friendship shared spoke, *He's the best friend you'll ever have.*

The warm spring breeze enwrapped us in Father's embrace.

And the glorious sunset speaks, *Your Father has an even better day ahead for you.*

We remember,

"No eye has seen,
no ear has heard,

no mind has conceived
what God has prepared for those who love him"
(1 Corinthians 2:9, NIV).

And we realize that in some ways that future has already begun.

Thanks for walking with me. I enjoyed your company. You needed to be imaginative to take this walk. I didn't because I often stroll this old path. But wherever *you* are, if you are observant, you can experience your Father's hugs in His creation. Even in the most desolate places His hugs are observable. And remember, these hugs from Heavenly Father are just the beginning. It gets much better than this.[3]

His Relational Hugs

For many of us, relational hugs feel especially satisfying. Sometimes these embraces come in the form of people literally putting their arms around us. At other times they come through caring words, kind acts, meaningful eye contact, facial expressions, body language, or simply being there when needed. For example, Heavenly Father's hugs may be experienced

when your two-year-old reaches his chubby arms
   around your neck,
when your four-year-old says, "I love you, Mommy,"
when your teenager does something special for your
   birthday,
when your grandchild runs excitedly to greet you,
when your spouse gives you that "I love you" look
   across a crowded room,
when a friend telephones to chat at just the right time,
when a stranger stops to help with your car trouble,
when . . .

Well, there's really no end to God's relational hugs, is there?

In the previous chapter, I mentioned there was more to the tear bottle story. It involves a relational hug from a friend.

You remember that I shared with the congregation the concept of a Heavenly Father who is emotionally involved with His children. I told them about Heavenly Father collecting our tears in His bottle. And I excitedly exhibited the 2,000-year-old tear bottle from the museum.

Here's the rest of the story. At the conclusion of the service, I was greeting people at the door. The line of friendly faces included an old friend, Duff Stoltz. Duff is a rugged individual—welder, builder, wood splitter, and outdoorsman. He works in security at the local hospital. He also is an outstanding church historian.

As he approached, Duff said, "Lloyd, you gave me a big hug today and now I have one for you." He threw his arms around my shoulders in a giant bear hug. I was blessed by his warm emotion. Then he added, "Somewhere in my collection, I have a genuine tear bottle. I want *you* to have it. Then you will always have one to demonstrate the love of our caring Father to other groups."

A few weeks later Duff located that ancient tear bottle and entrusted it to me. Since then, I've been sharing it with others. Thanks, Duff! Thank you, Father!

Sometimes Heavenly Father delivers His hugs through people who are close to us. At other times He gives them through strangers.

Last summer I finally delivered on a promise to my wife, Charlotte. All her life she had wanted to visit New Hampshire. Her family roots are in the little village of North Stratford. So we visited family sites. We entered the beautifully kept Baptist church and Charlotte sat at the organ her grandmother once played. We visited the house of her mother's childhood and the school her mother attended. We remembered her mother often mentioning the long two-mile walk to school through mountains of snow. Out of curiosity we measured the actual distance on the odometer. One-quarter of a mile! We shared a good laugh.

As the trip progressed, our car brakes started squawking. The noise grew louder and louder until eventually we had to arrange to have the brakes repaired. About thirty minutes before our scheduled appointment, we stopped to quickly grab something to eat.

We hadn't communicated very well. I thought I would run into the store and grab something to eat in the car. Charlotte intended to go into the snackshop. We jumped out simultaneously. I left the keys in the ignition. She hit the electric door lock. Immediately we knew we were in trouble. Locked out of the car far from home with an appointment for the brakes in a half hour.

A mechanic with the necessary tools came to help. But our car was especially difficult to unlock. After a half-hour struggle he gave up. We offered silent prayers and called someone else. It seemed like he worked on it for hours.

About then a group of bicyclists in their sporty outfits and safety gear pulled into the parking lot. Most of them went into the store for some refreshments. One young woman, helmet still in place, casually observed our plight.

Suddenly we heard a click and the mechanic said, "I've got it!" Immediately I heard a female voice say, "Praise the Lord!" And I thanked Him, too.

On the way to the brake shop, I commented on Charlotte's words of praise. "It wasn't me," she stated. The woman on the bicycle, a person we had never met, had delivered a special relational hug from Heavenly Father. Thank you, friend!

I believe one reason God uses many relational hugs is that many hurts come through *harmful* relationships. Many of His children have been wounded by others. So God often chooses to heal those wounds through His people. He asks

His sons and daughters to be His arms that wrap around His wounded children.[4] Thus we have the opportunity to be both recipients *and* deliverers of Heavenly Father's relational hugs.

His Dramatic Hugs

Then there are the more dramatic hugs. We often call them miracles. There are numerous biblical examples.

Jonah, the runaway messenger, couldn't escape God's hugs and the whale threw him up on the beach.

Daniel, staying true to his relationship with Heavenly Father, found that ferocious lions became household pets.

Shadrach, Meshach, and Abednego, who refused to bow to a false god, saw God stand with them in the furnace of fire.

Paul, repeatedly tossed in jail for proclaiming the Word, strolled out past sleeping guards and unlocking gates.

Joshua, fighting God's battle, commanded the sun to stand still. And daylight remained so he could finish the task.

And dramatic hugs still occur today. You might have experienced one yourself. Or at least observed one happening to someone you know.

There's Tom Ballard, who at age fourteen fell 350 feet down Crabtree Falls in Virginia. It was several hours before medics could reach him and six hours before he reached the hospital. Tom was unconscious for a week. His physician stated, "If he lives, he'll be a vegetable." Today, many years later, a very healthy Tom teaches government and history at a Christian high school in Maryland.[5]

There's Reynolds Price, a respected author who at age fifty-one had a malignant tumor along his spine. Following surgery and radiation treatment the physician said, "Six months to paraplegia, six months to quadriplegia, six months to death." Ten years later Reynolds is confined to a wheelchair. But he is very much alive and continues to write six days a week.[6]

There's Karolyn Herrmann, who for weeks desperately searched for a summer job to help with college expenses. A prayer group petitioned. Karolyn prayed. And she was offered a job. But not just any job. Her work was cataloguing scientific books—"A perfect job for an aspiring engineer."[7]

There's Ben Kent, three-year-old son of Wayne and Leslie Kent. A household accident tore Ben's trachea, causing air to escape from his lungs into his body. Ben nearly died several times in those first traumatic days. But there were praying congregations. And many people reaching out to Ben and his family with relational hugs from their Father. Six days after the accident Ben awoke. Now he is fully recovered.[8]

Of course, all difficult circumstances don't end so miraculously. We'll discuss those situations in chapter 15.

His Spiritual Hugs

Some of Heavenly Father's most important embraces are spiritual. As I write today, I am sitting at our dining room table. The landscape is covered by sparkling fresh-fallen snow. It reminds me of Father's love. I find myself praying with David, "Create in me a pure heart, O God, and renew a steadfast spirit within me" (Psalm 51:10, NIV). And because He is extremely forgiving,[9] my heart is washed clean. It is whiter than the snow.[10]

Forgiveness. Salvation. There is no better gift. There is no greater hug. "For God so loved the world that he gave his one and only Son, that whoever believes in him shall not perish but have eternal life" (John 3:16, NIV).

I don't need to point it out, do I? Probably not. But I'll feel better if I do. Who is it who loved the world? Who is it that gave us His Son? Our loving Heavenly Father, in concert with the Son and Holy Spirit, gave the best gift of all. Eternal life through Jesus Christ.

One of my favorite spiritual hugs is found in the creation story. "So God created man in his own image, in the image of God he created him; male and female he created them" (Genesis 1:27, NIV). His creating us was a wonderfully loving act. But He goes one step further. He makes us in *His* image! He gives us the capacity to think, to choose, to love, to hug, to procreate. . . . What wonderful hugs!

Then there is the wonderful hug of His love letter—the Holy Scriptures. They contain precious promises, stories about heroes of the faith, and the truth about who God is. What a unique gift He gave us. It is especially helpful to read the biblical record in light of the truth that Heavenly Father *is* love. It gives important perspective.

Heavenly Father's Word showers His affection . . .

For when you are lonely—

"So do not fear, for I am with you; do not be dismayed, for I am your God. I will strengthen you and help you; I will uphold you with my righteous right hand" (Isaiah 41:10, NIV).

For when you are in trouble—

"God is our refuge and strength, an ever present help in trouble" (Psalm 46:1, NIV).

For when you feel discouraged—

"What a wretched man I am! Who will rescue me from this body of death? Thanks be to God—through Jesus Christ our Lord!" (Romans 7:24–25, NIV).

For when you feel condemned—

"Therefore, there is now no condemnation for those who are in Christ Jesus" (Romans 8:1, NIV).

For when you face death—

"I am the resurrection and the life" (John 11:25, NIV).

Right along with the hugs contained in His Word are the loving embraces contained in prayer. Jesus taught us how to pray to God. He instructed us to address Him as "Our Father in heaven" (Matthew 6:9, NIV). Talking. Listening. Communicating with our Father. Meditating upon His Word. This privilege is certainly a wonderful heavenly hug.

A little counsel here might prove helpful. Don't always try to tell God just how and when to hug you. In other words, don't try to dictate to Him how He should express His love for you. To expect Him to answer our prayers exactly as *we* think He should is presumption—not faith. He is much wiser and much more loving than we will ever be. Trust Him to give you not merely what you *want*, but what you really *need*.

So enjoy His surprises! Watch for His hugs! If you are observant, you will be amazed at how many hugs He gives you. And you will be warmed by the realization of how much you are loved.

Would you like to go a step further? One of the greatest pleasures in life is to be a channel for Heavenly Father's hugs. If you want an extraordinary experience, become a messenger who delivers God's embraces. "We are therefore Christ's ambassadors, as though God were making his appeal through us" (2 Corinthians 5:20, NIV).

The opportunity to become a personal courier for Heavenly Father's hugs—what an honor!

We've briefly explored practical hugs, aesthetic hugs, relational hugs, dramatic hugs, and spiritual hugs. Undoubtedly there are many other ways Heavenly Father embraces us.

A cynic would say that if these are God's hugs, then all the negative incidents in our lives must be God's fist pounding angrily into our solar plexus. I see it differently.

We live in a world where we humans have given Satan

much control.[11] And "he prowls around like a hungry, roaring lion, looking for some victim to tear apart" (1 Peter 5:8, TLB). We live in a battleground. Not a playground. Sometimes I am amazed that God's hugs get through to us at all. But in spite of this world's chaos and sin, we still experience God's hugs. Especially if we alertly watch for them.

In a way, we are living in a concentration camp waiting to be freed. And if, as Corrie ten Boom discovered, the goodness of Heavenly Father (His hugs) can be found even in the hell of the Ravensbruck concentration camp,[12] His hugs can be found in your world, too.

Notes

1. See Matthew 7:9–11.
2. See Matthew 13:24–43.
3. See Revelation 21:1–5.
4. Henry Cloud and John Townsend, *False Assumptions* (Grand Rapids: Zondervan, 1994), p. 74.
5. Personal interview with an eye witness—my wife, Charlotte Erickson, February 2, 1995. Tom Ballard is her brother.
6. Reynolds Price, "Vision of Healing," *Guideposts* (August 1994), p. 2. John Skow, "Staring Down Loneliness," *Time* (May 22, 1995), p. 73.
7. Karolyn Herrmann, "What Prayer Can Do," *Guideposts* (June 1994), p. 33.
8. Wayne Kent, "Our Little Boy Was Not Alone," *Guideposts* (December 1994), p. 10.
9. See 1 John 1:9.
10. See Psalm 51:7 and Isaiah 1:18.
11. See Genesis 1–3.
12. Corrie ten Boom, John and Elizabeth Sherrill, *The Hiding Place* (Minneapolis: Worldwide Publications, 1971).

But when the fullness of time had come, God sent forth His Son, born of a woman, born under the law, to redeem those who were under the law, that we might receive the adoption as sons [and daughters]. And because you are sons [and daughters], God has sent forth the Spirit of His Son into your hearts, crying out, "Abba, Father!" Therefore you are no longer a slave but a son [a daughter], and if a son [a daughter], then an heir of God through Christ.

Galatians 4:4–7, NKJV (bracketed mine)

FIVE

The Father Who Never Abandons

We are sketching a profile of Heavenly Father, the God who wants us to live in His embrace. It is a profile drawn
carefully,
thoughtfully,
prayerfully, and we hope,
perceptively.
A profile I pray the Holy Spirit inspires as we seek the truth about Heavenly Father.

For some of you this process may be painful. It could bring back memories that hurt. But try to be patient and open to new perceptions. Because seeing who God really is will ultimately bring joy.

We have discovered that Heavenly Father is never too busy for His children. And that He is an emotionally involved parent. Now we contrast Him to a third type of parent in absentia—the *physically* absent father.

Human parents can be physically absent for many reasons—working long hours of overtime, working out of town consistently, doing their own thing, going off to war. Or divorce, illness, death.[1] Parents have control over some types of absences—but obviously not over all. With Heavenly Father there is *no reason whatsoever* that causes Him to be physically absent.

Steve was a macho-type guy in his thirties who came to a therapy group. He was terribly depressed. The first several sessions he stared at the floor. He never made eye contact. He never spoke. But slowly, almost imperceptibly, from session to session he began responding to the care demonstrated by group members. Within that safe environment, Steve allowed himself to begin experiencing deep emotions. Little by little his hard, uncaring exterior began melting.

Steve began to talk, at first expressing just small hints of his tremendous pain. Over time he shared how his father had abandoned him and his mother. Steve had been just eight years old. He described and reexperienced his intense feelings of rejection, pain, and anger.

He started realizing that his hard exterior was merely a protection from his deep pain and fear. By not permitting anyone to get close to him, he could never be hurt again. Now Steve began looking to the group for the nurturing, caring, and stability that he had so desperately needed from his father. It was the beginning of a long healing process.

Have you experienced a physically absent mother or father? If so, you know the pain. You know the emptiness. You know the agony of rejection. It hurts even now.

Or, for you, it could be the intense pain of being rejected by your spouse.

Or the loneliness caused by children who long ago seemed to forget that you exist.

Dear hurting friend, I have wonderful news for you. Is your Heavenly Father a physically absent parent? Has your Heavenly Father rejected you? Has He left you all alone? Absolutely not! Look at His promise: "The Lord will not abandon those who belong to Him; He will not forsake His people" (Psalm 94:14, CW).

Do you have difficulty believing this promise? Perhaps you have good reason not to trust parental promises.

Forty-year-old Shirley sat crying in my office. Her father had recently died and she was having an extremely difficult time coping with the loss. She sobbed, "But Dad promised me he'd never leave me. He promised me he wouldn't die."

What an improbable promise. Shirley's father could never fulfill it. He was human. Therefore he would die. And he did. Now Shirley had to deal with his death *and* his unfulfilled promise.

Perhaps your father made promises he didn't or couldn't keep. That would make it difficult for you to believe another Father's promises. Please, for your sake, take a fresh look at this Father. He is different than any parent you've ever known. Heavenly Father always keeps His promises because He *is* the Truth. And He is eternal. He will never die. He will always be physically present for you.

Many people have come to my office with abandonment issues. Some of these folk are youthful, some aged. For some the abandonment was real. For some, perceived. When these issues aren't resolved satisfactorily, they cause chronic problems with relationships. Problems relating to parents. Problems relating to spouses, children, friends, coworkers. And problems relating to Heavenly Father.

Barry was in his 60s. He was trim and physically fit. His graying hair and balding head gave him a distinguished and commanding appearance. With his wife, Karla, he came to my office. They came because their marriage was in trouble.

They had been married forty years, but most of those years had been difficult. Barry had a need to control virtually everything around him—his children, his colleagues, his friends . . . and Karla.

Karla had grown tired of being told where to shop, when to shop, what brands to purchase, which friends to see, and how long she could use the phone. Karla's individuality had been smothered for years. Now, somehow, she was finding the strength to assert some independence and occasionally express her own thoughts and feelings.

Karla's changes had challenged the status quo. Barry initially reacted angrily. Later he attempted to control through guilt. He wept bitterly, "You just don't love me anymore. Why don't you love me the way you used to?" Translated: *Why don't you think the way I want you to think and do what I want you to do?*

Perhaps a pause for some personal reflection would be helpful here. In your relationship with God, have you been like Barry? Think about it. Have you tried to control God and how He might relate to you? I must confess that I have. Perhaps you have, too. "Father, if You will just get me this job, I'll believe in You." Or, "I'll do anything You ask if You will just heal my baby."

Most of us at some point in our Christian experience have prayed this type of prayer. Sometimes it's a little more subtle. Sometimes it's more sophisticated. But we've prayed that way. We've attempted to manipulate God.

When you stop to think about it, what an ignorant and futile attempt that is! Heavenly Father is too great, too wonderful, and too loving to be controlled or manipulated. To attempt telling Him how He should express His love toward us is not only inappropriate—it is arrogant.

Back to Barry and Karla. As I counseled them, I noted that many changes had occurred in Barry's life in recent years. Their son and three daughters one by one had left to make homes of their own. At work Barry had been passed over for promotion after promotion. He said it was because of his age. I guessed there were other reasons—such as his need to control others. Finally, in disgust, he had taken an early retirement.

Barry, who needed to feel in control, was losing control. The last straw was Karla wanting to make some of her own decisions.

In therapy we explored Barry's early life and found that he had good reasons for his fear of abandonment. We looked at what he knew about his adoption. He believed his birth-parents had not wanted him. "So they got rid of me," he sobbed. He was adopted into a home where little affection was expressed and much was demanded of him. Never did he feel fully accepted. He always had to prove himself.

As an adult Barry attempted to control situations so he couldn't get hurt again. In his desperate attempt to keep from being abandoned once more, he clung so tightly that people pushed away from him. The more desperate he became, the more people needed to escape his clutches. Barry's fear of abandonment caused tremendous problems in his life.

Friend, you may have been disappointed by your parents, spouse, children, friends, or church leaders. They may have hurt you. They may even have abandoned you. But you have never been abandoned by your Heavenly Father. If you thought so, that abandonment was in your perception. It was not based on reality. At the beginning of our world, it was not God who left our first parents.[2] And it's not He who leaves relationships today.

> Never will I leave you; never will I forsake you (Hebrews 13:5, NIV).

> When my father and my mother forsake me, then the Lord will take care of me (Psalm 27:10, NKJV).

Can it get any clearer? Could He be any more specific? *He will not leave you!*

You are Heavenly Father's child. In fact, you are Heavenly Father's child twice. You are His by creation and you are His by adoption.

"For as many as are led by the Spirit of God, these are the sons [and daughters] of God. For you did not receive the spirit of bondage again to fear, but you received the Spirit of adoption by whom we cry out, 'Abba, Father' " (Romans 8:14–15, NKJV, bracketed mine).

You are so much Heavenly Father's child that you can call Him "Daddy." That's what it says. *Abba* is Aramaic for *dearest father.* We would say *Daddy.*

Aramaic was the common language used by Jesus. The term *Abba* is found only three times in Scripture. Twice it tells us that since Heavenly Father adopted us, we can call Him "Daddy." The other time Jesus addressed His Father in the Garden of Gethsemane, " '*Abba*, Father,' he said, 'everything is possible for you. Take this cup from me. Yet not what I will, but what you will' " (Mark 14:36, NIV).

Hours later Jesus experienced the separation that clinging to sin ultimately causes. He hadn't sinned. But He took our sins upon himself.[3] He thus experienced separation from His Father. It's why He cried, while agonizing on the cross, "My God, my God, why have you abandoned me?" (Matthew 27:46, The Message). Jesus and His Father endured separation so that we could graphically see where sin leads when it remains unforgiven and unhealed. They endured this suffering so that we will never need to experience such terror and pain.

If your childhood memories include feelings of rejection and abandonment, hang on to this truth. If your childhood memories include words and actions from less than perfect parents—that's all of us—hang on to this truth. You are Heavenly Father's child by creation. You are Heavenly Father's child by adoption. You are His *twice.* He is a fantastic parent. And you have the right to call Him "Daddy."

Perhaps, as you've been reading, you've questioned, "How can He be a *physically* present Father? I can't see Him." That's a good question.

I believe that we get too dependent upon our physical eyes. Many things exist that we can't see. Odor, heat, cold, sound, gases, ideas, memories.

Have you ever headed toward the bathroom during the night and stubbed your toe on the bedpost? As you danced the dance of joy, did you have any doubt about the reality of the bedpost? None at all! You couldn't see the bedpost, but you certainly discovered its existence.

Just so with Heavenly Father. We currently cannot see Him with our physical eyes. But that doesn't mean He is physically absent. We can still hear His voice with our inner ears. We behold Him in His Word. We observe Him at work in our lives. We see Him through His creation. We sense His presence. And we can feel His warm hugs.

Many of my illustrations have contrasted human parenting to the heavenly variety. But there are many positive examples of wonderful Christian parenting that mirror God's character. I'll tell you about two of them.

The first is a young grieving father. Kevin came home from his office one afternoon and found a note on the table. His wife of ten years was divorcing him. When Kevin initially came to my office, we processed his shock. Then we worked on his deep feelings of loss and rejection.

Soon Kevin began focusing on the children and how they would be affected by the divorce. He decided that he would do everything possible to keep his children. I tried to provide comfort and support as Kevin waged the battle for his son and two daughters.

Kevin faced the loss of friends (who seem to take sides in divorce situations). He faced a financial crisis. He faced the embarrassment of numerous false accusations. He faced an in-depth court investigation. Finally, he faced the judge herself. Incredibly, Kevin was awarded physical custody of his children.

Sherrie is the second parent who refused to abandon her child. She and her policeman husband had a beautiful baby daughter. But Sherrie's husband was physically abusive and would beat the child. When Sherrie attempted to protect her daughter, she received his fury.

Sherrie left home with her daughter numerous times. In spite of a divorce, her husband always managed to find them and force them to return. He beat them savagely. The daughter was becoming a physical and emotional wreck. So was Sherrie. Sherrie knew she must do something.

There seemed to be no safety for her child in the judicial system. In desperation, Sherrie broke the law and fled from the state. She's still a fugitive. She has no money and can't get public assistance. She survives on a minimum wage job. Sherrie has done all this for the sake of her child. She protects her daughter at all costs.

Two parents. One a father. One a mother. Both, in extremely difficult circumstances, refusing to abandon their children. This is the kind of parent Heavenly Father is.

This is the type of Parent you have. He will never forget you. Listen to what He tells you. "I have engraved your name on the palms of my hands. You are always in my thoughts. How can I forget you?" (Isaiah 49:16, CW).

Your name is written on Heavenly Father's hands. *Your* name is in Heavenly Father's mind. It is. It is. He will never forget your name. And He will never forget you.[4] "Can a woman forget the baby she feeds at her breast? Will she not have compassion for the new life that has come from her womb? Yes, it's possible that she may forget or abandon her offspring, but I will never forget or abandon you. You are mine" (v.15).

You are twice Heavenly Father's child.
He will never forget you.
    He will never abandon you.
        Never.[5]

Notes

1. In "Life Without Father," *USA Weekend* (February 24–26, 1995), David Blankenhorn argues that fathers are an endangered species. The following statistics based on the Unites States census are offered as proof of "disappearing dads."

U.S. children living with	1960	1980	1990
Mother and father	80.6%	62.3%	57.7%
Mother only	7.7	18.0	21.6
Father only	1.0	1.7	3.1
Father and stepmother	0.8	1.1	0.9
Mother and stepfather	5.9	8.4	10.4
Neither parent	3.9	5.8	4.3

2. See Genesis 1–3.
3. See 2 Corinthians 5:21.
4. With appreciation to Max Lucado, *When God Whispers Your Name* (Dallas: Word Publishing, 1994), p. 2.
5. See 2 Corinthians 4:8–9, TLB.

Every good and perfect gift is from above, coming down from the Father of the heavenly lights, who does not change like shifting shadows.

James 1:17, NIV

But every good endowment and every complete gift must come from above, from the Father of all lights, with whom there is never the slightest variation or shadow of inconsistency.

James 1:17, Phillips

Six

The Model of Consistency

Human beings have difficulty being consistent. When we do something incompatible with our values we say, "Well, I'm only human." Sometimes our only consistent quality is our inconsistency. Is it any wonder that our parenting is also inconsistent?

There are many types of parental inconsistencies. Some parents have wild mood swings. Some give mixed messages to their children. Some give preferential treatment to one child. Some scapegoat a child.

Some parents have inconsistent expectations. Some have erratic limits for their children. Some have unsettled disciplinary procedures. And the words of some parents are incompatible with their actions ("Do as I say, not as I do").

In profiling Heavenly Father's consistency, let's examine just two types of consistencies—consistent boundaries and consistent mood. These two characteristics are interrelated because they both are expressions of His love.

Parenting specialists have written prolifically about the importance of parents providing consistent limits or boundaries for their children.[1]

As children grow older, the limits must be expanded. The limits must be well understood by parent and child. And the boundaries must be consistently enforced.

Parental structure produces a sense of comfort and security for the child. Dr. James Dobson says, "There is security in defined limits."[2]

Barb grew up in a home with well-defined limits and consequences. Her parents were as consistent as humanly possible. Barb often wished her Saturday night curfew would be extended so she could stay out later with her friends. Sometimes she even wished she could attend her friends' parties with their free-flowing alcohol.

Years later, Barb told me, "Looking back on my growing-up years, I now really appreciate the limits my parents set for me. I see what's happened to my friends. Although I sometimes voiced frustration, underneath I was pleased that my parents cared enough to *not* give me everything I wanted. I knew I was loved. And I knew what to count on. In retrospect, I wouldn't have wanted it any other way."

In Rick's home *consistency* was a foreign term. Family members came and went at will and with little communication. His parents were either working, partying, or sleeping. Rick had no limits. No caring. No nurturing.

As an adult, Rick still searches for a sense of belonging. He is insecure and unhappy. He floats from job to job, from relationship to relationship, and from bar to bar. He's still looking for the security and happiness that eluded him during childhood. He can't relate to job requirements. He can't maintain his responsibilities. His life is, in a word, inconsistent.

Heavenly Father knew about our need for consistent limits long before we psychologists "discovered" it. That's why He gave us clear boundaries. He wants us to feel secure and loved and He wants to protect us from getting hurt. He is a Father who cares enough to provide boundaries.

Therefore, He told Adam and Eve not to eat from a certain tree in Eden. They were safe, secure, and supremely happy until they crossed Heavenly Father's boundaries and followed Satan's deceptive lies. Then they felt so miserable that they didn't even want to have their daily walk and talk with Heavenly Father.[3]

Heavenly Father gives all His children limits. (Yes, limits are a gift.) We are to worship only the true God. We should not make idols of worship. We need to be respectful in using God's name. We are to keep His day holy. We are to honor our parents. We are not to murder, commit adultery, steal, lie, or covet (Exodus 20:3–17). Jesus summarized these boundaries. " 'Love the Lord your God,' He said, 'with all your heart and with all your soul and with all your mind.' This is the first and greatest commandment. And the second is like it: 'Love your neighbor as yourself.' All the Law and the Prophets hang on these two commandments" (Matthew 22:37–40, NIV).[4]

Even though we have repeatedly overrun Heavenly Father's boundaries, these limits are extremely important to us. We need *consistent* boundaries. They play a vital part in providing our security and happiness. Scripture counsels, "Stay always within the boundaries where God's love can reach and bless you" (Jude 21, TLB).

Wouldn't it be a wonderful life if each of God's children always stayed within His boundaries? It certainly would save much heartache and pain. But like our own children, we are tempted to think that boundaries are set up to inhibit our happiness. Like our children, we have ventured outside of Heavenly Father's boundaries.

Thankfully, Heavenly Father is consistently forgiving.[5] And He provides the power for us to stay within the boundaries in the future.[6]

Because we all grew up with some degree of parental inconsistency, it may be difficult to see Heavenly Father as consistent—as Someone you can always count on. But I encourage you to listen to His words:

> For I am the Lord—I do not change" (Malachi 3:6, TLB).

> But every good endowment and every complete gift must come from above, from the Father of all lights, with whom there is never the slightest variation or shadow of inconsistency (James 1:17, Phillips).

Let's focus now on a second type of parental inconsistency—erratic moods.

Jack worked extremely hard to provide for the needs of his family. He and his wife, Jennifer, bore four children in the first five years of their marriage. Jen stayed home to care for them.

Jack worked third shift (11:00 P.M. to 7:00 A.M.) in a large cereal manufacturing plant. In spite of earning good wages, he was hard-pressed financially. He volunteered for overtime whenever it was offered. He often worked ten-hour shifts and at least one day on the weekend. Sixty-hour work weeks became commonplace. This schedule eventually exhausted Jack, making him irritable and resentful.

Jennifer tried to quiet the children so Jack could sleep when he arrived home from work in the morning. But children are children and when their play awoke him, he exploded. "Shut up and play somewhere else!" The verbal assaults caused the children to be frightened and confused.

In those rare times when Jack was well rested, he treated his children with love and concern. But most of the time, tension and anger polluted the atmosphere of their home.

The children walked on eggshells because they didn't want to upset Dad and risk his wrath. They just weren't sure about him. They didn't know what to expect. Jack's attitude toward them was inconsistent.

Perhaps you can relate to the experience of Jack's children. Or to some other inconsistent parental attitude or mood.

Do you remember waiting for your father to be in a "good mood" before asking to borrow the car? Or perhaps you waited until after you had finished the dishes before asking your mother if you could stay overnight at a friend's house. I did it. You probably did it. Our children still do it.

With Heavenly Father this tactic is unnecessary. He is in a perpetually good mood regarding His children. There is no time He is unapproachable. He always wants us to communicate our feelings and thoughts. In fact, He so much desired to restore our lost relationship that He sent His Son on a search, find, and rescue mission. Because of Jesus we once again can have direct access to our consistently loving Heavenly Father.[7] "Ask and it will be given to you; seek and you will find; knock and the door will be opened to you. For everyone who asks receives; he who seeks finds; and to him who knocks, the door will be opened" (Matthew 7:7–8, NIV).

Heavenly Father is not moody. He doesn't bring home a bad attitude from work. He doesn't take His frustrations out on His children. He is stable. He's as solid as a rock.[8]

Like His Son, Heavenly Father is "the same yesterday and today and forever" (Hebrews 13:8, NIV).

Sometimes it's impossible for us to fully comprehend

Heavenly Father's consistent kindness and love. It's difficult to perceive how He could possibly be constantly caring

> when we hear about the slaughter of innocent people in central Africa or eastern Europe.
> when we learn about the most recent city to be crumbled by an earthquake or cyclone.
> when we read about the family dispute in our neighborhood that caused the death of a child, or
> when still another friend tells us that she has cancer.

During those moments it's important to remember that we are human beings—sinful human beings. As such, we "see through a glass darkly,"[9] and it's impossible for us to always see His consistency. That does not mean that He is inconsistent. It simply means that we cannot *see* His consistency. We are much like the small child who can't possibly comprehend the thinking of his parents. (We will discuss that further in Chapter 15.)

With our distorted vision and limited understanding, we may sometimes perceive inconsistency in Heavenly Father. But I believe that if we were blessed with heavenly vision, we would see a crimson cord stretching through every event in our lives. If we could but see clearly, we would see His consistent love.

One day soon it will be made clear. We will observe that through it all, Heavenly Father's love has been constant.[10]

His treatment of all His children has been consistent.

His concern for our well-being has been unwavering.

His hatred of sin because of what it does to His daughters and sons has been unfailing.

And we are constantly on His mind. "How precious it is, Lord, to realize that you are thinking about me *constantly!* I can't even count how many times a day your thoughts turn toward me. And when I waken in the morning, you are still thinking of me!" (Psalm 139:17–18, TLB, italics mine).

Heavenly Father consistently thinks of our well-being.

His loving attitude toward us is constant. He always cares enough to give us loving boundaries. He always grieves when His love is rejected by one of His children. He always rejoices when we respond positively to His love.[11]

That's the way He is.

Always.

You can count on it.

Notes

1. See Bruce Narramore, *Parenting With Love and Limits* (Grand Rapids: Zondervan Publishing House, 1987), and James Dobson, *The New Dare to Discipline* (Wheaton, Ill.: Tyndale House, 1992).
2. James Dobson, *Dare to Discipline* (Wheaton, Ill.: Tyndale House Publishers, 1970), p. 42.
3. See Genesis 3:8–10.
4. Jesus was actually quoting Old Testament scripture with which He was so familiar. See Deuteronomy 6:5 and Leviticus 19:18.
5. See 1 John 1:9.
6. See 2 Peter 1:3–4.
7. See Luke 19:10; 1 Timothy 1:15; Hebrews 4:14–16; 7:25; 10:22.
8. See Genesis 49:24; Deuteronomy 32:4; 2 Samuel 22:2; Psalm 18:2.
9. See 1 Corinthians 13:12.
10. Ibid.
11. See Luke 15.

He forgives all my sins. He heals me. He ransoms me from hell. He surrounds me with lovingkindness and tender mercies. . . .

He is merciful and tender toward those who don't deserve it; he is slow to get angry and full of kindness and love. . . . He is like a father to us, tender and sympathetic to those who reverence him. For he knows we are but dust, and that our days are few and brief, like grass, like flowers, blown by the wind and gone forever.

But the lovingkindness of the Lord is from everlasting to everlasting, to those who reverence him; his salvation is to children's children of those who are faithful to his covenant and remember to obey him!

Psalm 103:3–4, 8, 13–18, TLB

SEVEN

Defender of the Defenseless

It may be difficult to understand how anyone could view Heavenly Father as abusive. It might even sound irreverent. Conversely, it may be virtually impossible to perceive Him as nonabusive.

If you haven't had personal experience with abuse, be grateful. This topic is extremely painful for many of Heavenly Father's children. As you contemplate this subject, apply Scripture's counsel, "Suffer with them as though you were there yourself" (Hebrews 13:3, TLB).

If you had the misfortune of being abused as a child or youth, it would be natural to think of authority figures as abusive. Especially if you were mistreated by your father, you will tend to see Heavenly Father as abusive.

Most Christians can readily recognize abuse when it occurs in human families. What we're slower to realize is that we may have a profile of an abusive Heavenly Father. For example:

What do you call it when a human parent leaves young children to fend for themselves? The abuse of neglect. Yet that's exactly how many Christians see Heavenly Father—uninvolved and removed from their daily lives.

What do you call it when a human parent strikes a child every time the child does something the parent doesn't approve of? Physical abuse. Yet many Christians see Heavenly Father as a parent who will clobber them if they step out of line.

What do you call it when a parent fastens her children in their car seats and pushes the car into a lake? Abuse. Murder! Yet many Christians see Heavenly Father as causing the earthquakes, tornadoes, war, and airplane crashes that take the lives of His children.

Is Heavenly Father abusive? Could it possibly be? Is He like the human parent who may have abused you?

Human parental abuse comes in many forms—verbal, emotional, physical, sexual, spiritual, and neglectful. In all cases the desires or wants of the parent take precedence over the basic needs of the child. The child, as a result, suffers incredible pain—not only at the time of the abuse but for a lifetime.

Research statistics within Christianity are startling. Seventy-eight percent of sexual molestation occurs in homes claiming to be religious.[1]

Research and clinical observation have also found that the more rigid the religious values demanded by a denomination, the more likely that sexual molestation will occur within that church.[2]

A recent study of members belonging to a conservative Christian church found that of those responding to a mailed survey—thirty percent had been physically abused at home before age eighteen, forty-three percent were verbally/emotionally abused at home before age eighteen, and sixteen percent experienced incest at home before age eighteen.[3]

There can be no doubt but that child abuse is common. And that the emotional consequences are devastating to the victim.

This topic is particularly difficult for me to present. I know that many of the readers of this book have been hurt by abusive parents. You've lived all your life with that pain. I really don't want to inflict any more anguish. Unfortunately, there are still people who don't believe that abuse exists—especially in the church, in Christian schools, or in the homes of dedicated churchgoers. So I must give a couple of true examples. If this is too painful for you, skip to the next line break, where we will observe a Father who is not hurtful.

Julie came for psychotherapy for a number of years. Her painful depression was so intense that she required hospitalization several times. Why was this thirty-year-old in such distress?

When Julie was an early adolescent her father began abusing her sexually. He forced her to perform unspeakably degrading acts. Then, perhaps to assuage his own guilt, he threw her into a closet and yelled at her to seek forgiveness for her sins. At other times he insisted that God could never love her—she was too wicked, too sinful, too damaged to be worth saving.

What terrible treatment of a youthful child of God. Unfortunately, it gets worse.

Julie's father was an official in their church. He often led the congregation in long, fervent prayers. And Julie observed.

Is it any wonder that this precious child of Heavenly Father has immense difficulty picturing Heavenly Father as loving and kind? Is it any wonder that she has confused feelings about Heavenly Father?

What a travesty of parenthood. What a betrayal of Christian responsibility. What a diabolical profile of Heavenly Father. He is portrayed as Satan truly is. And Satan gloats.

Thirteen-year-old Sherry lived in an adolescent residential treatment center. She had previously experienced much neglect and emotional abuse in her home. Sherry had attempted to fill her needs for caring and nurturing in unhealthy ways—through alcohol and sex. When her parents left the state, they didn't even tell her where they were going.

Sherry did have one thing going for her, one person who cared for her—a wonderful Christian counselor.

One cold November night the telephone rudely awoke this therapist at 2:00 A.M. There was an emergency. The therapist rushed to the center and discovered Sherry on the roof of a four-story building. Sherry was screaming and cursing and threatening to jump. She had been up there awhile, and the situation was growing desperate.

Intuitively the psychologist shouted, "Sherry, you're coming to my house for Thanksgiving. Come down now!" Sherry stopped screaming, came down from the roof, went to her room, got into bed, pulled the blankets over her head, and went to sleep.

The therapist knew that most of the residents were soon leaving on passes to spend Thanksgiving with their families. Since Sherry had been disowned, she was lonely and desperate. What Sherry needed right then was a loving parent substitute.

I wonder. How many Sherrys are there in your world? How many people are there who need someone to demonstrate what Jesus intended to convey when He invited us to call God our Heavenly Father?

Is Heavenly Father abusive? The answer seems obvious. But to be certain, let's take a look at the actions of the One who is most like Him.

Joash was born on the wrong side of the tracks. He was a hated foreigner. In spite of this disadvantage, he experienced a pleasant life. He had a nice home and loved his beautiful wife and two young children.

But one day Joash noticed that his hands didn't feel quite right. Then a sore appeared that wouldn't heal. At first he wouldn't allow himself to believe the devastating truth. *It couldn't be happening to me, could it?* But it was. Joash was eventually diagnosed with a very contagious disease.

In those days the treatment of choice was harsh—lifetime banishment. He was forced to leave his family and live in a shanty outside of town. Joash became an outcast and had to scavenge for food.

Wherever he went he was forced to shout, "Unclean, unclean!" And people scattered to avoid being near him. Occasionally he caught a distant glimpse of his family. How his arms ached to hold his children. How his heart longed for the companionship of his wife.

It wasn't just the leprosy that was destroying him. People, even his former friends, viewed his disease as a punishment from God for some great sin he must have committed. Even Joash believed it.

How did Jesus treat this man who had been so misused by his church, family, and community? As Jesus was entering his village, Joash and nine fellow lepers asked Him for mercy. "When he saw them, he said, 'Go, show yourselves to the priests.' And as they went, they were cleansed" (Luke 17:14, NIV).

Joash ran back to thank Jesus. He was so grateful.

Grateful that Someone didn't despise and mistreat him.

Grateful that Someone had rescued him from the pit of emotional and spiritual abuse.

Grateful that Someone had returned him to his place in

his family and community.

Grateful that Someone had restored his self-respect.

That's how Heavenly Father treats His children who have been abused.

No, Heavenly Father is not an abusive parent. He has a very tender heart. He hurts when His children are in pain. And He gets angry when someone abuses His children.

"And whoever welcomes a little child like this in my name welcomes me. But if anyone causes one of these little ones who believe in me to sin, it would be better for him to have a large millstone hung around his neck and to be drowned in the depths of the sea" (Matthew 18:5–6, NIV).

Strong words! But Heavenly Father has strong love for His children—especially those who are young or otherwise defenseless. Heavenly Father is the precise opposite of an abuser. He defends the abused. Just as Jesus stood with the defenseless, Heavenly Father sides with those who are abused today.[4] And He will ultimately rescue His abused children.

There is absolutely no reason to fear Heavenly Father. He loves you so much. His love for you is perfect.

"We need have no fear of someone who loves us perfectly; his perfect love for us eliminates all dread of what he might do to us. If we are afraid, it is for fear of what he might do to us, and shows that we are not fully convinced that he really loves us. So you see, our love for him comes as a result of his loving us first" (1 John 4:18–19, TLB).

As a good Parent, Heavenly Father does provide needed discipline.[5] But He is *never* abusive.

As a loving Parent, He may work to bring some good out of a tragedy. But that does not mean that He caused the tragedy.

Heavenly Father loves you deeply and perfectly. He would never do anything to harm you. In fact, He has gone to incredible lengths and taken immense risks to rescue you from the one who is the abuser.

What a compassionate Parent He is!

Notes

1. David T. Ballard, et al., *A Comparative Profile of the Incest Perpetrator: Background Characteristics, Abuse History, and Use of Social Skills* in *The Incest Perpetrator*, Anne L. Horton, Barry L. Johnson, Lynn M. Roundy, Doran Williams, eds. (Newbury Park, Calif.: Sage Publications, 1990), p. 50.
2. William H. George and G. Alan Markatt, *Introduction* in *Relapse Prevention With Sex Offenders*, D. Richard Laws, ed. (New York: Guilford Press, 1989), p. 10. Lynn M. Roundy and Anne L. Horton, *Professional and Treatment Issues for Clinicians Who Intervene With Incest Perpetrators* in *The Incest Perpetrator*, Anne L. Horton, Barry L. Johnson, Lynn M. Roundy, Doran Williams, eds. (Newbury Park, Calif.: Sage Publications, 1990), p. 187.
3. Fred Kasischke and Audray Johnson, *Adventists & Family Crises: Getting the Facts* (Adventist Review, August 18, 1994), p. 17.
4. See Matthew 21:12–15.
5. See Proverbs 3:12; Hebrews 12:5–6.

What can we ever say to such wonderful things as these? If God is on our side, who can ever be against us? Since he did not spare even his own Son for us but gave him up for us all, won't he also surely give us everything else?

Who dares accuse us whom God has chosen for his own? Will God? No! He is the one who has forgiven us and given us right standing with himself.

Who then will condemn us? Will Christ? No! For he is the one who died for us and came back to life again for us and is sitting at the place of highest honor next to God, pleading for us there in heaven.

Romans 8:31–34, TLB

EIGHT

The Nonperfectionistic Perfect Parent

Bonnie's parents fought incessantly. Her father was alcoholic, irresponsible, and demanding. Her mother worked hard to hold the family together. She worked full time and did all she could to please her husband.

When Bonnie was ten, her father had a stroke that left him physically dependent. Bonnie was the oldest child and already had been largely responsible for her siblings. Now she also bore the burden of caring for her unhappy father. She waited on him constantly. She even had to help him bathe and take care of his bodily functions.

Father had always been difficult to please. But now, no matter how much Bonnie did, he demanded more. No matter how carefully she performed her task, it wasn't good enough. No matter how much she was there, she wasn't there enough.

At age fifteen Bonnie met a boy who said he loved her and she left home. Although they were young, they worked hard to make a success of their lives. Working hard was something Bonnie knew how to do.

Bonnie finished high school and had two children. But she wasn't happy. She wanted more. She returned to a full-time job. She still wasn't happy. So she added college classes to her already heavy schedule.

Bonnie had high goals. But when she accomplished them, she realized little satisfaction.

It was never enough.

She had internalized her father's impossible-to-please attitude. She continues attempting to earn approval and acceptance. Bonnie expects much of herself and those around her. When her expectations aren't met, she gets depressed.

Many Christians view Heavenly Father as exceedingly difficult to please—demanding, critical, perfectionistic, condemning. They do everything possible to try to please Him. Still, they feel that they don't measure up to His expectations.

Is this an accurate profile? Let's take another look at the One whose attitude and actions best represent Heavenly Father.

Jesus grew up surrounded by perfectionism. He lived in a condemning Pharisaical environment.

Nicodemus was one of those Pharisees—perfectionistic and critical. He was unsatisfied and unhappy (as are all perfectionistic Christians). Was Nicodemus an evil man? Quite the contrary; he was one of the best men in Israel. He lived his religion.

But something was missing in Nicodemus' life. His belief was, *Obey and you will earn God's love. Do what God asks and He will have to include you in His kingdom.* Nicodemus had become quite good at it. But not good enough.

One night Nicodemus sought time alone with Jesus. Jesus looked into his heart and soul. He said, "I tell you the truth, no one can see the kingdom of God unless he is born again" (John 3:3, NIV).

Nicodemus, you believe you are doing all the right things. You think you are on the way to the kingdom. But you are all mixed up. Your good deeds will never get you into my kingdom. What you need is a new heart.

What a relief it is to discover that we cannot obey God with the nature we are born with.[1] No one can. It can't be done. When we understand that fact, we can fall helplessly before Heavenly Father and say, "OK, here I am. Show me your love."

Nicodemus didn't fully respond to Jesus that night. But later when he saw Jesus on the cross, he understood. He realized how much he was loved—even though he didn't deserve it. There was nothing he had done, or could do, to earn Heavenly Father's love. That love was already his.

Before his conversion Nicodemus believed that obedience won Heavenly Father's love. Now he knew that Heavenly Father's love wins trust and obedience. He had believed that righteousness brings salvation. Now he understood that salvation brings righteousness.

Friend, if you picture a critical Heavenly Father, pay close attention to what Jesus told Nicodemus. "For God did not send his Son into the world to condemn the world, but to save the world through him" (John 3:17, NIV).

What good news! He doesn't condemn. Instead, through His Son, Heavenly Father rescues. Condemnation doesn't save. Love saves.

Who then is the condemner? It is the devil, Satan. Scripture calls him "the accuser of our brethren" (Revelation 12:9–10, KJV).

Some people would argue that Heavenly Father must be perfectionistic because Jesus said, "Be perfect, therefore, as your heavenly Father is perfect" (Matthew 5:48, NIV). Doesn't that sound perfectionistic?

Perhaps at first glance. But do you think Jesus would ask

us to do something that is impossible? We were *born with* carnal (sinful) natures. So we can't be perfect—unless we claim Jesus Christ's perfection.

Only by accepting His perfect life can we obtain perfection and salvation. He didn't ask us to do the impossible. He did it for us.[2]

A group of Pharisees once set a trap to see if Jesus agreed with their profile of a critical Heavenly Father.[3] They created a situation so they could catch a woman in the act of adultery. They knew this woman, and it was an easy task to get the required number of witnesses.

They grabbed this unsuspecting woman and threw her at the feet of Jesus. They were seeking the death penalty. (By the way, these Pharisees were so hypocritical that they didn't accuse the male adulterer. Where was he? Might he have been one of them?)

The woman clutched her blanket tightly around her and gazed at the dirt a few inches from her face. She knew her fate was sealed. Her view of Heavenly Father was the same as the Pharisees. That's exactly why she was doing what she was doing. She felt so helpless, so hopeless, so utterly unloved.

Quietly Jesus bent down and began writing in the dirt. I'd love to know what he wrote, wouldn't you? Perhaps He wrote the sins of the Pharisees. "If," He said, "any one of you is without sin, let him be the first to throw a stone at her" (John 8:8, NIV).

How their faces must have blanched with humiliation. One by one they shuffled away until Jesus was alone with the woman.

He stood up and asked, "Where are your accusers? Has no one condemned you?"

For the first time, the woman dared look up. Hope was returning. She realized her accusers had vanished and she responded, "No one, sir."

And Jesus, representing His Father, said, "Then neither do I condemn you." What relief and joy must have flooded her heart!

How could Jesus be so magnanimous? How could He *not* condemn her?

He had come to rescue and save. Not condemn.[4] He knew that very soon He would bear the brunt of Satan's condemnations on the cross.[5] He loved this woman so much that He willingly accepted the condemnation she deserved.

Then Jesus said, "Go now and leave your life of sin." How could He make such a seemingly impossible command?

For the first time in her life this woman had experienced love. Love set her free from the bondage of sin. What she had been looking for in the street she found in the heart of Jesus Christ.

Tina is a modern counterpart of this woman. She had been a high school friend of the pastor. It had been years since he had seen her. One day she unexpectedly arrived on his doorstep.

Tina looked worn and tired. She had dark circles under her eyes and her hair was unkempt. "Come in, Tina. What brings you here?"

As Tina sat in the warm hospitality of the pastor's living room, she began to weep.

"My life is such a mess. I don't know where to go. As a child I was sexually abused by my father. And for some reason, I've developed an obsession with sex. I can't control my urges. Every few days I find myself out on the street. It doesn't matter who it is. Lately I've been running into some pretty rough guys. If I don't change my life, I'll soon be dead. Can you help me?"

The pastor and his wife looked at each other. Their gaze asked one question, *What would Jesus do?*

"We'll do our best to help you. You can stay with us.

We love you." They prayed with Tina and asked Heavenly Father to show her His love.

Tina had a sexual addiction. Could it be changed instantaneously? Not normally.

Tina thought of herself as dirt and expected everyone else to view her the same way. Every few days she'd dress for the street. The pastor and his wife tried to tell her she was much too valuable for that. But Tina could only cry and say, "I don't know how to help myself." And off she'd go.

One night Tina returned very shaken. "Do you think angels go with me when I'm out on the street? I was taught that God's angels leave me when I don't do what He wants."

The pastor responded, "Heavenly Father knows you want to be free. He has not abandoned you."

Tina related that she had picked up a couple guys. They started getting violent and pulled a knife. They told her to drive to a certain secluded spot.

"I knew that if I drove there my life was over. I was terrified. Then it seemed like a voice whispered in my ear, 'Speed up.' And I sped up. 'Now run into that telephone pole.' And I sped right into the pole."

"We were all shaken. A crowd gathered and those rough guys ran off."

Tina concluded her experience, "I'm home, I'm home! God saved my life. Do *you* think God saved my life?"

"Of course He did. Don't you know how much He loves you?"

"No, I don't know. Tell me again."

And the pastor had the privilege of telling Tina the story of Jesus and the adulterous woman. He told her that Heavenly Father doesn't condemn her; He wants to save her.

They all cried and prayed together that night. Over the next few weeks God changed Tina's life.

Every time Tina's compulsion came, she fell to her knees. Instead of praying, "Jesus, I promise not to sin," she prayed, "Jesus, love me some more." And Heavenly Father's love filled her great need to be loved and turned her away from her addiction.

In the process of healing, Tina was welcomed into a warm, nurturing church family. She also worked with a Christian psychotherapist.

It has been several years since that fateful night. Tina remains satisfied with the love of Heavenly Father. She no longer feels that she's not good enough. She knows Heavenly Father as a loving, accepting Parent.

Friend, if Jesus didn't denounce the woman thrown at His feet, if God didn't condemn Tina, then Heavenly Father isn't critical of you either. There is no salvation in condemnation. Heavenly Father's love, not our obedience, brings salvation.[6]

How did Heavenly Father demonstrate His great love? How did He show us that He forgives rather than condemns? How did He prove that He knows sinful humans cannot be perfect?

Rather than letting us face the final consequences of choosing to sin, Heavenly Father sent His Son on a rescue mission. Jesus came "to seek and to save what was lost" (Luke 19:10, NIV). He came and lived perfectly *for* us. And He suffered *for us* the consequences that sin dishes out. When we accept His gift of salvation, we *are* perfect—in Christ.[7]

So . . .

"Who dares accuse us whom God has chosen for his own? Will God? No! He is the one who has forgiven us and given us right standing with himself.

"Who then will condemn us? Will Christ? No! For he is the one who died for us and came back to life again for us and is sitting at the place of highest honor next to God, pleading for us there in heaven" (Romans 8:33–34, TLB).

Heavenly Father is not perfectionistic, critical, or judgmental. He is accepting, forgiving, caring, and nurturing.

This Parent is on *your* side.

That's why He sent His Son.

And that's why we call Him Savior.[8]

Notes

1. See Romans 7:14–25 and Romans 6:8–21.
2. See Hebrews 12:2; 10:10–12; Acts 4:12.
3. See John 8:2–11.
4. See John 3:17.
5. See Isaiah 53:3–6.
6. See John 3:16.
7. See Acts 4:12; Romans 1:16–17; 1 Thessalonians 5:9–10; 1 John 4:16–17; John 3:16; 14:6; Hebrews 10:19–23.
8. With appreciation to Dale Leamon. Several thoughts expressed in this chapter are based upon sermons he presented in Battle Creek, Michigan, January 28 and February 4, 1995.

But now, this is what the Lord says—he who created you, O Jacob, he who formed you, O Israel: "Fear not, for I have redeemed you; I have summoned you by name; you are mine."

Isaiah 43:1, NIV

NINE

Merciless or Merciful?

Jeremy was a seminary student having difficulty with several of his professors. As we talked I discovered that there had been problems wherever he went. He couldn't relate to people.

The primary problem was Jeremy's anger. He was frustrated with the church he was co-pastoring, irritated with his teachers, upset with his girlfriend, and unhappy with living in Michigan.

We explored his early life and discovered that this young seminarian had been raised in a dysfunctional home. His father was an extremely angry man. Jeremy had endured much emotional and physical abuse.

As an adult Jeremy was mad at the world. He was defensive and sensitive. Not surprisingly, he viewed God as a very angry Person. Jeremy lived in fear of God's wrath.

Are you afraid of Heavenly Father? I'm not asking about respect, reverence, or a sense of awe—the type of fear often referred to in Scripture. I'm asking about raw fear. Perhaps terror. Do you see Heavenly Father as an angry, harsh, vindictive Person? Be honest. Search your heart.

Through the years many of God's children have felt terrorized by God. Israel often trembled with fear at the Lord's actions.[1] In the Middle Ages Christians did penance and went on long pilgrimages to appease what they believed to be an angry God. In early American history, ministers like Jonathan Edwards preached such dramatic "hellfire and brimstone" sermons that listeners fainted from fright.

Even today it is not uncommon to hear Christians talk of a harsh, angry, judgmental God. Heavenly Father is sometimes perceived as Someone trying to find things wrong with us so He can keep us out of heaven.

What a horrible profile of Heavenly Father. It's the picture the devil wants us to have. Unfortunately, Christians have given the devil a lot of help. So have some parents.

Susie was sixteen years old when she was first brought to me for counseling. Initially she was a resistant client. She wouldn't talk. But as we gently worked, her breaking heart overflowed.

She discussed how her mother had died a year before. Susie had experienced intense pain and loneliness. In her grief she had searched desperately to replace her mother's love and care. She got mixed up in the wrong crowd. Smoking marijuana seemed to numb her pain.

Susie's father discovered what she was doing. When she came home from school one day, he and several of her older siblings were sitting in the living room. He was furious and said, "Pack your things. You're going to live with Jill and Bob." Jill was Susie's married sister.

He didn't tell Susie why he was so angry. Tearfully she packed and left the only home she had ever known.

Susie's heart had been shattered. She had not only lost her mother, but now her father and her home as well.

Thankfully, as therapy progressed the father became willing to get involved in the process. He worked on some of his own pain. Slowly, as their wounds healed, they grew together.

A delightful memory for me is Susie and her father walking from my office and down the sidewalk—hand in hand. Susie's face was beaming. This was her father and she was basking in his love. No more anger. No more pain or fear.

Unlike Susie's father, Heavenly Father is *always* nurturing, forgiving, and loving. Never has He been harsh or vindictive with us.

"I have loved you with an *everlasting* love; I have drawn you with loving-kindness" (Jeremiah 31:3, NIV, italics mine).

"Let him have all your worries and cares, for he is *always* thinking about you and watching everything that concerns you" (1 Peter 5:7, TLB, italics mine).

In profiling Heavenly Father as the warm, forgiving individual He is, I think of David. This time David is not a pseudonym but the David you know in Scripture.

When God chose David to be the king of Israel, He called him "a man after my own heart."[2] David became a great king and accomplished many good things. But there were times when he was anything but godly.

One evening he went to the roof of his palace and observed the beautiful Bathsheba bathing.[3] He sent someone to find out about her and discovered that she was married to one of his loyal soldiers who was at the battlefront. David was so smitten by her beauty that he sent for her anyway and committed adultery with her.

When Bathsheba became pregnant, David grew desperate. First he called Uriah back from battle and attempted to get him to go home to Bathsheba for a conjugal visit. David hoped Uriah would then think the child was his. But Uriah was so loyal to David that he refused to take time off. The desperate king arranged to have Uriah killed in battle.

Adultery.

And murder.

Did Heavenly Father get angry with David's behavior? Surely. Because Uriah and Bathsheba were also His children. Heavenly Father hates sin and what it does to His people. He must have been very upset (a "baptized" word for angry) that Uriah and Bathsheba were treated so cruelly.

Did God's anger mean that He was harsh and vindictive with David? Was He unwilling to forgive? Did He stop loving David? Not at all.

When David was unrepentant, God sent Nathan the prophet to point out his sins. Though it took time, David's response was, "I have sinned against the Lord." And he sought and obtained forgiveness.

Years later David died and his son Solomon ascended to the throne. God came to Solomon in a dream and said, "Ask for whatever you want me to give you" (1 Kings 3:5, NIV). Solomon responded, "Give your servant a discerning heart to govern your people and to distinguish between right and wrong" (1 Kings 3:9, NIV).

Heavenly Father was pleased with his response and promised Solomon much more. He concluded, "If you walk in my ways and obey my statutes and commandments *as David your father did*, I will give you a long life" (1 Kings 3:14, NIV, italics mine).

Years later, in the days of King Jeroboam, God made a similar statement about David. He "kept my commandments and followed me with all his heart, doing only what was right in my eyes" (1 Kings 14:8, NIV).

On both occasions Heavenly Father stated emphatically that David had kept His commandments. There was no mention of David's adultery or murder. Heavenly Father looked at David as though He had never sinned.

This doesn't mean that Heavenly Father doesn't get angry. He does. Heavenly Father gets angry when someone or something harms His children.[4]

He gets angry when someone presents an untrue picture of Him and leads His children away from Him.[5]

He gets angry at injustice and mistreatment.[6]

But Heavenly Father doesn't stop loving because He is angry. His anger is not harsh or vindictive. He calls the offender to repentance. He is not willing that anyone should perish.[7]

Heavenly Father demonstrated His patient love for David. And David responded with total love and commitment to God. He prayed, "I seek you with *all my heart*; do not let me stray from your commands" (Psalm 119:10, NIV, italics mine).

David wasn't satisfied with a knowledge about Heavenly Father. Neither was he content with a casual relationship with Him. Only a wholehearted living relationship would do.

Once I presented this story of God's loving treatment of David to a congregation. As I shared Heavenly Father's full and complete forgiveness of David, I noticed the eyes of a middle-aged woman begin to water. As I continued with the beautiful truth of Heavenly Father's kindness and love, tears streamed down her face.

After the service she asked to speak with me privately. She related that for twenty years she had been carrying a heavy burden of guilt over an extramarital relationship.

She was a Christian but she hadn't comprehended how Heavenly Father could possibly forgive her. She had perceived Him to be angry with her for her actions. That's how her human father had always treated her.

Now her tears expressed relief and joy. How unburdened she was when she discovered that Heavenly Father wasn't still angry with her. What great joy she felt in experiencing Heavenly Father's mercy. She realized that she had no reason to fear Heavenly Father.

"Fear not, for I have redeemed you; I have summoned you by name; you are mine" (Isaiah 43:1, NIV).

Friend, Heavenly Father is not harsh and vindictive with you—no matter what you may have done. He lovingly calls you by name and there is no reason to fear Him.[8] Come to Him and He will treat you as compassionately as He did David.

"Let us then approach the throne of *grace* with confidence, so that we may receive *mercy* and find *grace* to help us in our time of need" (Hebrews 4:16, NIV, italics mine).

> Gracious
> Merciful
> Compassionate
> Patient
> That's your Heavenly Father!

Notes

1. See Exodus 19:16.
2. See 1 Samuel 13:14 and Acts 13:22.
3. See 2 Samuel 11–12.
4. See John 2:13–17.
5. See Luke 9:51–56 and Matthew 23:13–39.
6. See Luke 13:10–17 and Matthew 21:12–17.
7. See 2 Peter 3:9.
8. See Isaiah 41:9–10.

Endure hardship as discipline; God is treating you as sons [and daughters]. For what son [or daughter] is not disciplined by his [or her] father? If you are not disciplined (and everyone undergoes discipline), then you are illegitimate children and not true sons [and daughters].

Moreover, we have all had human fathers who disciplined us and we respected them for it. How much more should we submit to the Father of our spirits and live! Our fathers disciplined us for a little while as they thought best; but God disciplines us for our good, that we may share in his holiness.

No discipline seems pleasant at the time, but painful. Later on, however, it produces a harvest of righteousness and peace for those who have been trained by it.

Hebrews 12:7–11, NIV (bracketed mine)

TEN

He Cares Enough to Discipline

Rick and Sharon were blessed with four beautiful children. Unfortunately, their home was chaotic. They were extremely busy with work and graduate school. But the real problem was the absence of parental authority. No teaching or correction was occurring.

The children fought, screamed, and cried. There was little parental response until one parent exploded. Then the children behaved well for a short time.

Sharon and Rick's overindulgence was understandable. They had both grown up in dysfunctional homes.

Rick had experienced a lack of discipline due to negligent parenting. His parents had confused permissiveness with love. This was the only way Rick knew to parent.

Sharon's parents had been punitive and harsh in their "discipline." She was determined that she would never "discipline" her children.

So the children floundered without guidance.

Eventually Sharon and Rick realized that they had a problem. They became involved in counseling to deal with their individual issues.

They also attended parenting classes and discovered that true discipline is neither harsh nor permissive. The word *discipline* is related to the word *disciple*. Disciples are not made by yelling at people. But neither are they made by neglecting their training. As with Jesus, people become disciples through thoughtful, caring teaching. The purpose of true discipline is to teach.

Christian family specialists indicate that permissive parenting is a mistake.[1] An undisciplined child doesn't learn to respect authority, doesn't learn to control his impulses, and doesn't develop positive self-esteem. Contrary to some popular psychology, discipline in its pure form is good parenting.

Rick and Sharon learned that when parents overindulge a child, it usually is meeting a need of the parent. It is seldom beneficial for the child. Permissiveness fills two parental needs: (1) taking care of one's self (providing discipline is hard work) and (2) approval (some parents can't tolerate their children not liking them—even for a few minutes).

It was extremely difficult for Rick and Sharon to change long-standing family patterns. But as they applied basic principles of discipline, slowly their home became less chaotic. Respect for one another prevailed.

Rick and Sharon discovered the biblical concept that "these commands are a lamp, this teaching is a light, and the corrections of discipline are the way to life" (Proverbs 6:23, NIV).

They attempted to model their parenting after their heavenly Parent. They discovered that He is a loving Parent, not an overindulgent Parent. He loves too much to give His children everything they want. "My son, do not despise the LORD's discipline and do not resent his rebuke, because the

Lord disciplines those he loves, as a father the son he delights in" (Proverbs 3:11–12, NIV).

Pastor Ellison ministered in one of the largest congregations in the Southwest. He was an extremely personable and effective pastor. His television ministry flourished and he was in demand as a speaker across the country.

His church grew rapidly. He became involved in building projects and organizing various shepherding and outreach ministries. Other pastors sought his secrets of church growth.

Pastor and Mrs. Ellison had two sons, Hal and Phil. While Pastor Ellison shepherded his congregational flock, he did not lead his own lambs. The parents hesitated to correct their sons because it took too much of their precious time and energy. The boys learned little about the ways of God and they developed no respect for others or themselves.

Hal and Phil grew into manhood. Surprisingly, they remained in the church. But they didn't stay to obtain or give spiritual blessings. They were filled with rebellion and brought the devil to church.

They manipulated to obtain important church positions. Their work in the treasurer's office and with the deaconry provided the opportunity to steal from the church and its parishioners. Over the years they stole thousands of dollars. Their work in youth ministry allowed them to mingle with the young people—especially young women—and become sexually involved with several of them.

The behavior of these self-centered, self-indulgent young men became well known in the congregation. Members became discouraged and stopped attending. Someone eventually summoned the courage to present the problem to Pastor Ellison. He acted surprised and hurt. In reality, he already knew what his sons were doing. He just hadn't been able to bring himself to discipline them.

With his congregation confronting him, Pastor Ellison finally was forced to speak with his sons. But by now they had no respect for their father, the church, or God. They paid no attention to his mild rebuke and continued in their sins.

Sound familiar? You've probably read about Pastor Ellison before. His real name is Eli.[2] Eli, the priest and judge at Shiloh, was a permissive parent. He failed to provide the needed discipline for his sons Hophni and Phinehas.

Even doing church work didn't excuse Eli from providing the discipline his own children needed. Because of his negligence, Eli lost his church, his sons, the ark of the covenant, and his life. Negligent parenting indeed has a high price.

The principles of love and discipline are not contradictory. In fact, love often demands discipline. Love says "no" when "yes" isn't in the best interests of the child. Truly loving parents don't give in to every whim of their child. *Parental* discipline is necessary in the process of teaching *self-*discipline.

You may have grown up with little or no correction and teaching. Or you may have grown up with belligerent so-called "discipline." Either way, it may be difficult to conceptualize discipline being helpful. But it is.

"Those whom I love I rebuke and discipline. So be earnest, and repent" (Revelation 3:19, NIV).

Moses had studied at the feet of the most learned professors in the Royal University of Egypt. He graduated at the head of his class from the Royal Military Academy. To human eyes no one ever looked so ready to lead a people. But Moses still needed to attend Heavenly Father's University of Faith.

He had to repeat the four-year graduate program ten times before he was ready to lead God's children. He had to learn to be a shepherd before he could be a general.

In the wilderness Moses learned the lesson of faith. He learned to submit his plans to Heavenly Father. He learned patience and humility. He learned that a good spiritual leader *follows* Heavenly Father. He learned submission and obedience to Someone greater and wiser than he.

Have you experienced Heavenly Father's discipline? He may not send you to the wilderness, but . . .

you may not get the promotion you cherish,
you may not be healed of the physical malady that
    plagues you,[3]
you may not retain the church office you have enjoyed,
your manuscript may be rejected for publication,
attendance at the Bible study group you lead may be less
    than recordbreaking.

If so, don't worry. You are building a solid character in Heavenly Father's University of Faith.

Does Heavenly Father's discipline sometimes confuse you? It can be difficult to differentiate between Heavenly Father's discipline and the devil's harassment. To add to our confusion, Heavenly Father can sometimes bring something good out of the tragedies Satan causes.[4] And Satan can wreak havoc with some of the good things God gives us.[5] Then add the natural consequences that occur because of our own choices and actions. The one thing we do see clearly is that we lack 20/20 spiritual vision.

Although it may take study and prayer to discern what is happening, one basic principle continually applies. Satan's desire is to harm and ultimately destroy us.[6] Heavenly Father's goal in discipline is to help and finally save us.[7]

That's an important reason Heavenly Father gave us the Scriptures—to guide us to salvation. Discipline is part of His work in us.

"All Scripture is God-breathed and is useful for teaching, rebuking, correcting and training in righteousness, so that the man of God may be thoroughly equipped for every good work" (2 Timothy 3:16–17, NIV).

Good human parents realize that appropriate discipline is necessary and helpful for the growth of their children. Could we expect any less of Heavenly Father?

"Our fathers disciplined us for a little while as they thought best; but God disciplines us for our good, that we may share in his holiness. No discipline seems pleasant at the time, but painful. Later on, however, it produces a harvest of righteousness and peace for those who have been trained by it" (Hebrews 12:10–11, NIV).

What a blessing it is to have a Heavenly Father who isn't so permissive that He leaves us to our own folly.

He cares enough to discipline.

He treasures enough to teach.

He cherishes enough to "point out" (rebuke).

He reveres enough to confront.

He loves enough to risk being misunderstood.

Thank you, Father.

Notes

1. Bruce Narramore, *Parenting With Love and Limits* (Grand Rapids: Zondervan Publishing House, 1987), pp. 38–39. James Dobson, *Dare to Discipline* (Wheaton, Ill.: Tyndale House, 1970), pp. 40–41.
2. See 1 Samuel 2:12–36; 4:10–18.
3. See 2 Corinthians 12:7–10.
4. The story of Job is a good example.
5. Marriage, for example.
6. See 1 Peter 5:8.
7. See Luke 19:10.

The mind of sinful man is death, but the mind con-
trolled by the Spirit is life and peace; the sinful mind is
hostile to God. It does not submit to God's law, nor can
it do so. Those controlled by the sinful nature cannot please
God.

Therefore, brothers [and sisters], we have an obliga-
tion—but it is not to the sinful nature, to live according to
it. For if you live according to the sinful nature, you will
die; but if by the Spirit you put to death the misdeeds of
the body, you will live, because those who are led by the
Spirit of God are sons [and daughters] of God.

Romans 8:6–8, 12–14, NIV (bracketed mine)

ELEVEN

The Issue of Parental Control

Jamie was distraught. Her mother had phoned with the news that she planned to attend Jamie's graduation from graduate school.

Jamie and I had been working for several months on problems related to overcontrolling parents. A new crisis now emerged.

"My parents always controlled my life," Jamie told me. "They made all my decisions for me. Recently, I've been gaining some independence. But now Mom's coming. I'll have to mom-proof the house."

"What do you mean 'mom-proof' your house?" I asked. (I knew about child-proofing but hadn't heard of mom-proofing.) "Mom is always telling me what to do or how I could have done something better. She snoops everywhere. I'll have to hide everything of a personal nature—telephone bills, telephone numbers, letters, work applications, classwork, car payments, utility bills. I'll put it all in a locked box under my bed. When Dad was alive they both ran my life. Now that it's just Mom, she tries to control me enough for both of them. *I'm tired of them controlling my life!"*

Jamie capably expressed the cry of many adults controlled by their parents. While many people suffer from father hunger, many others long to be freed from an overcontrolling, overinvolved parent.

Parents can control through finances, weakness, fear, shaming, negative reaction, intimidation, or manipulation.[1] These parents don't feel good about themselves. They have an intense fear of abandonment. In their desperation they do whatever it takes to maintain a dominating adult/child relationship.[2]

The church appears to have more than its share of overcontrolling parents. Perhaps because most Christian parents are truly concerned about the eternal well-being of their children. They also may be concerned with appearance. If their children make bad choices, they feel embarrassed, guilty, judged—like failures.

In many cases overcontrolling parents are admired for their "sacrificial involvement." Christian parents are often able to get away with such parenting under the guise of "love."

But overcontrol leads to deteriorating relationships. The adult child rebels against the parents and everything they stand for. Or the adult child becomes overly submissive, showing no mind or character of his own—easy prey for strong-willed, authoritative leaders.[3]

Some people see Heavenly Father as overcontrolling and dominating. Have *you* ever wished that He would go away and stop smothering you with His demands?

There's a wonderful Garfield Valentine card that perceptively portrays this view. The cartoon cat holds his heart in his paw and demands, "It's your choice . . . love me or leave me!" When the card is opened, Garfield threatens,

"Make the wrong choice and I'll break your arm!"

"Be my Valentine, or I'll break your arm." Is this an accurate profile of Heavenly Father? Does He *demand* love? Does He insist that we do things His way?[4]

A basic premise of Scripture is that Heavenly Father created us free moral beings.[5] He gave us intelligence and the power of choice. If He hadn't, we would be robots—with no ability to think, to decide, to love.

Remember Judas? For three years Jesus taught him by word and example. Jesus tried to influence Judas to make positive choices.

Note carefully that Jesus did not exclude Judas simply because He knew Judas was heading in the wrong direction. Neither did He intimidate or manipulate him. Instead He continued ministering to Judas. At the Last Supper, He even washed his feet. But ultimately He allowed Judas' decision to become the betrayer.[6] How hard that must have been for Jesus.

And how hard that must have been for Heavenly Father—to see one of His children betray His only begotten Son. But He didn't intervene. He didn't overcontrol. What respect He must have for the free will of His children.

Tammy and Jon's eight-year marriage was in trouble. Jon felt that the "significant other" in Tammy's life was her mother—not himself. In a way, he was correct.

Once I returned a telephone call to Tammy regarding an appointment. Instead of saying "hello" when she picked up the phone, Tammy said, "Mother . . ." This simple incident suggested an enmeshed relationship.

Tammy had been convinced by her mother that she was incapable of being a good parent—that she needed her mother's help. No baby-sitters for this couple. Only Tammy's mother was qualified.

In this way, Tammy's mother controlled when Tammy worked, slept, and shopped. She controlled where Tammy and Jon lived (on her beautiful acreage) and how much time they had for themselves (almost none).

Jon felt miserable and was beginning to find courage to say so. Tammy also was miserable but she wasn't as aware of it. Unless changes were made, their marriage was doomed.

Barry was overcontrolled by his father through finances and intimidation. He was forty-five years old and had worked at the family business since high school. He had developed excellent management skills but had no self-confidence.

No matter what Barry did, it wasn't good enough for his father—the company president. Barry was anxious and unhappy. He hated his job.

I asked why he didn't leave and start his own business.

"Oh, I could never do that. I'd fail for sure. At least here I have a regular income."

Here was a big, strong 220-pound man who was still being controlled by his sixty-eight-year-old father.

Is Heavenly Father like Tammy's mother? Or Barry's father?

Is He like Garfield? Does Heavenly Father threaten to break the sinner's arm? Is He so controlling that He threatens to torture and kill those who won't love Him? Here is good news—especially if you've been plagued by an over-controlling parent.

Heavenly Father has no desire to control His children through threats or any other means. Intimidation may gain behavioral compliance, but it destroys relationships. Remember that "God is love" (1 John 4:16, NIV). And that "There is no fear in love. But perfect love drives out fear, because fear has to do with punishment. The one who fears is not made perfect in love" (1 John 4:18, NIV).

The ultimate demonstration of Heavenly Father's respect for our individuality is that He will finally let go of any child who insists on going his or her own way. He

doesn't want to lose any of His children[7] but He will ultimately respect the sinner's wishes. He will give them up.[8]

Although He has complete knowledge of what is good
for us, Heavenly Father *still* does not impose His will. He
allows us the character-building privilege of making
choices.

Heavenly Father persuades but He doesn't coerce.

He urges but He doesn't compel.

He convinces but He doesn't force.

He won't break your arm.

And He doesn't kill.

At the cross the sinless Jesus was viewed as a sinner. But
it was not Heavenly Father who killed Him.[9] And He won't
torture or kill any of His children who remain sinners.

It's sin that kills.

"Sin pays its servants: the wage is death" (Romans 6:23,
Phillips).[10]

Sin cannot exist in the presence of Heavenly Father's
glory.[11] Could it be that the glorious fire that brings salvation to the redeemed is the same fire that consumes those
who remain in sin?[12] Probably. We know for sure that the
death of the wicked is no arbitrary act on the part of Heavenly Father. From the very beginning He warned us that
sin causes death.[13] But how we relate to Heavenly Father
and His glory is up to us.[14]

As Heavenly Father watches His rebellious children die,
He will weep over the loss of His beloved sons and daughters.

> *How can I give you up, my son?*
> *How can I let you go, my daughter?*[15]

Just as surely as a human parent grieves over the loss of
a child killed by the child's drunk driving, Heavenly Father
will weep. He grieves even now when we make choices that
are harmful to our relationship with Him.

"As surely as I live, declares the Sovereign LORD, I take no pleasure in the death of the wicked" (Ezekiel 33:11, NIV).

Heavenly Father has gone to extreme lengths to save us from the results of sin.[16] Let's not blame the physician for our illness. If we refuse the antidote, sin will kill us. But the choice *is* ours.

Control is not always a dirty word. It is entirely appropriate for a parent to restrain a toddler from running into the street. Appropriate control becomes overcontrol when the parent is still restraining the child long after she is capable of making such decisions on her own.[17]

Heavenly Father exercises prudent control by telling us what is good for us. He points out the results of bad choices because He doesn't want us to get hurt.[18] But He doesn't force us to follow His directives. Instead, He hopes that we will learn to love and trust Him so much that His instruction becomes part of us:

> My son [daughter], do not forget my teaching, but keep my commandments in your heart, for they will prolong your life many years and bring you prosperity. Let love and faithfulness never leave you; bind them around your neck, write them on the tablet of your heart. (Proverbs 3:1–3, NIV, bracketed mine)

> I will put my laws in their minds and write them on their hearts. I will be their God, and they will be my people. (Hebrews 8:10, NIV)[19]

In one sense we desperately need Heavenly Father's control. Without it we are powerless against sin and death.[20]

We are powerless to change our hearts.

We are powerless to control our impulses and thoughts.

We are powerless to purify our lives.

But, we can choose to have Him do those things in us.

We can choose to accept His antidote.

We can choose to follow His directions.
We can choose to love and trust Him.

"Not by might nor by power, but by my Spirit, says the Lord Almighty" (Zechariah 4:6, NIV).

Our salvation and growth in Christ are certainly not accomplished by our pitiful strength. Not even by Heavenly Father's incredible power. But by the loving, persuading influence of the Holy Spirit.

No arm-twisting here! Just the voice of the Spirit—
    usually quiet and still,[21]
sometimes boisterous and dynamic (to get our
    attention),[22]
always sent by a loving Father.

"For if you live according to the sinful nature, you will die; but if by the Spirit you put to death the misdeeds of the body, you will live, because those who are lead by the Spirit of God are sons [and daughters] of God" (Romans 8:13–14, NIV, bracketed mine).

The choice is yours and mine. Love cannot be commanded. Trust cannot be coerced.

What a wonderful Father He must be to have created us with the capacity to make decisions.[23]

What a caring Father He must be to provide the remedy for our sinful decisions.[24]

What an incredible Father He must be to ultimately honor our decisions.[25]

Controlling? Yes. At your invitation. For your good. For your salvation.

Overcontrolling? Not this Father. Not Heavenly Father. He loves you too much.

Notes

1. H. Norman Wright, *Always Daddy's Girl* (Ventura, Calif.: Regal Books, 1989), p. 127ff.
2. Susan Forward, *Toxic Parents* (New York: Bantam Books, 1989), pp. 70–71.
3. Ross Campbell, *How to Really Love Your Child* (Wheaton, Ill.: Victor Books, 1977), p. 68.
4. With appreciation to Graham Maxwell, *Servants or Friends?: Another Look at God* (Redlands, Calif.: Pineknoll Publications, 1992), p. 19.
5. See Genesis 3:1–24.
6. See John 13:10–30.
7. See 2 Peter 3:9.
8. See Romans 1:18–32, RSV or NEB.
9. See 2 Corinthians 5:21; Romans 4:25; John 10:17–18; 1 Peter 2:24.
10. See also 1 Corinthians 6:9–11; Galatians 5:19–21; Ephesians 5:1–5; Revelation 21:27; Genesis 2:17; 3:19; Romans 5:12; 6:21; 1 Corinthians 15:21–22, 55–56.
11. See Exodus 33:18–23; 1 John 3:2–6; 1 Timothy 6:15–16.
12. See Matthew 25:41; Isaiah 33:14–15; Exodus 24:17; Daniel 7:9–10; Ezekiel 28:14; 2 Thessalonians 2:8.
13. See Genesis 2:17.
14. For a more complete discussion of this concept see Graham Maxwell's *Servants or Friends?*
15. See Hosea 11:8, TLB.
16. See John 3:16.
17. Forward, p. 50.
18. See Deuteronomy 10:12–13.
19. See also Ezekiel 36:26; Hebrews 10:16; 2 Corinthians 3:1–3.

20. See 1 Corinthians 15:12–31; Ezekiel 18:4; Romans 3:1–31.
21. See John 3:6–7; 1 Kings 19:9–13; Revelation 3:20.
22. See Exodus 19:16–19.
23. See Deuteronomy 30:11–20.
24. See Proverbs 3:5–6; John 3:16.
25. See Revelation 22:11.

How great is the love the Father has lavished on us, that we should be called children of God! And that is what we are!

1 John 3:1, NIV

TWELVE

Perfect Love, Perfect Father

Ben grew up longing for a close relationship with his parents. It wasn't that they didn't love him. They said they loved him very much.

When Ben made them feel proud, his parents showered him with warmth and affection. But most of the time they were cold and aloof. They said they wanted to encourage him to excel, and their parenting style appeared to work when Ben was a young boy. He did anything and everything to obtain the approval of his parents. As he grew older, however, he began to feel that his parents didn't really love *him*. He concluded that they only loved what he could do for them.

Ben grew into a teenager and his love for his parents became a mirror image of his parents' love. He had learned well how to love conditionally. He excelled at school and sports only when his parents did something to please him.

This pattern continued for several years. In time, neither

Ben nor his parents expressed love to each other. They all waited for the other to do something rewarding. Resentment and anger abounded.

What Ben had learned was *I'll love you if you excel and make me feel good*. His parents' love was based on conditions. Ben could not possibly excel all the time. He learned to feel hopeless. Depression set in.

Eventually, Ben's depression prompted the family to seek help.

Have you experienced conditional love? A foolish question, I know. Much of what passes for love is based on conditions. A better question may be: Have you experienced unconditional love?

This chapter really shouldn't be necessary. But it is. When Scripture says "God is love" (1 John 4:8, NIV), that says everything.

Unfortunately, the word *love* has been so adulterated that it contains little of its intended meaning. Permissiveness, harshness, infatuation, overcontrol, selfishness, conditional approval—all masquerade as love. The devil has severely corrupted "love."

The type of "love" we're most familiar with has qualifiers. Perhaps the love you received from your parents had conditions attached.

I'll love you *if* you clean your room.

I love you *when* you get good grades.

I love you *because* you're so cute.

But Heavenly Father loves you *anyway*. With Him there are no qualifiers.

Margaret was a sixty-five-year-old grandmother suffering from chronic depression. For years she had kept her feelings bottled up. In one of her first sessions she said, "I'm a rock. *I am a rock*. Nothing gets to me."

Indeed, her emotions were frozen. But as therapy progressed, her hardness slowly melted and she permitted herself to experience the pain locked deep inside.

Margaret had been an unwanted child. When she was born there were already five children in this impoverished family. Besides, Margaret was different. She used the term "homely."

"Everyone made fun of me—even my parents. Dad said my nose was as big as the Washington monument. I just needed to be loved and I didn't know what I had done wrong."

Sobbing with grief, Margaret concluded, "I didn't look good enough for my father. And he didn't love me. He told the other kids that he loved them but he *never* said that he loved *me*."

What a contrast to Heavenly Father, who loves us even in our ugliest, most selfish, most unlovable moments.

Peter was so self-confident. Even cocky. "Lord, I am ready to go with you to prison and to death" (Luke 22:33, NIV). Imagine his confusion when Jesus told him that before the rooster crowed in the morning, he would disown Jesus three times.[1]

A few hours later, as Peter was denying that he knew Jesus for the third time, the rooster crowed. Jesus "turned and *looked* straight at Peter" (Luke 22:61, NIV, italics mine). And Peter remembered. He rushed out of the building and wept bitter tears of self-contempt, remorse, and repentance.

What was it about Jesus' look that prompted Peter's response? Tenderness, compassion, forgiveness, love. And it came at one of Peter's worst moments. Peter realized how much he was loved.

Do you remember the story of the adulterous woman thrown at Jesus' feet? She received this look and was forgiven.[2]

Do you remember David the adulterer and murderer? He received this look and Heavenly Father stated that David had always kept His commandments.[3]

Do you remember . . . you? Yes, YOU! You have received this look. No matter what you have done, or said, or thought, Heavenly Father looks at you with compassion and forgiveness. You can't do anything to make Him stop loving you. He can't keep from loving you. It is part of Him. For "God *is* love."

Remember "Jesus loves me"—the children's song? You probably learned the words as a child.

> "Jesus loves me! this I know,
> For the Bible tells me so;
> Little ones to Him belong,
> They are weak but He is strong.
> Yes, Jesus loves me!
> Yes, Jesus loves me!
> Yes, Jesus loves me!
> The Bible tells me so."

He does. And so does His Father. Did you learn this verse?

> "Jesus loves me when I'm good,
> When I do the things I should."

Okay, I know you're with me so far. But can you believe the concept expressed in the next two lines?

> "Jesus loves me when I'm bad,
> Even though it makes Him sad.
>
> Yes, Jesus loves me!"[4]

He does. He certainly does. And so does Heavenly Father. Even when we hurt Him. Even when we disappoint Him. Even when we reject Him. His love truly is unconditional.

We often refer to 1 Corinthians 13 as the "Love Chapter." These verses also tell us a lot about Heavenly Father.

Since He *is* love, the descriptions of love also describe Him. Thus, we can arrive at the following conclusions about Heavenly Father.

"*Heavenly Father* is patient,

Heavenly Father is kind.

He does not envy, *He* does not boast, *He* is not proud.

He is not rude, *He* is not self-seeking, *He* is not easily angered, *He* keeps no record of wrongs.

Heavenly Father does not delight in evil but rejoices with the truth.

He always protects, always trusts, always hopes, always perseveres.

Heavenly Father never fails" (1 Corinthians 13:4–8, NIV, italics mine).

What a beautiful description of Heavenly Father. And His love.

There really is no question about Heavenly Father's love for us. That was settled at Calvary. The more compelling question is this: How will we respond to His love?

It's true that He will love us whatever our response. If we decide against Him, He will still love us. That's the kind of person He is. His attitude toward us is not dependent upon our response to Him.

While His love is guaranteed, our salvation isn't. Our eternity depends on our response. He will never stop loving us, but He cannot save without a positive response from us.

How do you know if you truly love Him?

It was Mother's Day. I was eleven years old and feeling guilty because I hadn't purchased Mom a card.

Weekends were always hectic for Mom. She worked full-time outside the home so her two sons could have a Christian education. Weekends were catch-up time. For her, Mother's Day was little different from any Sunday.

I wanted to do something to let Mom know that I loved her. Going to the kitchen where she was baking bread, I said, "Happy Mother's Day. I love you, Mom."

She smiled a weary smile and said, "That's nice. I love you, too." I was about to escape with that when she added, "If you love me, you could show it by washing the dishes."

I honestly can't remember my response. I hope I did the dishes.

In my immaturity, I thought that love was composed of nice words and warm feelings. Mom was teaching me that genuine love is that—and much more. It is demonstrated in our actions.

That's what Jesus was teaching us when He said, "If you love me, you will obey what I command" (John 14:15, NIV).

The apostle John elaborated, "But if someone who is supposed to be a Christian has money enough to live well, and sees a brother in need, and won't help him—how can God's love be within *him?* Little children, let us stop just *saying* we love people [or Heavenly Father]; let us *really* love them, and *show it* by our *actions*" (1 John 3:17–18, TLB, bracketed mine).

Jesus concluded, "Love the Lord your God with all your heart and with all your soul and with all your mind and with all your strength" (Mark 12:30, NIV).

Love Him with your entire being. With your words, your thoughts, your feelings, and your actions. The actions come—not to earn Heavenly Father's love but because you already are loved by Heavenly Father.

That's the response His love deserves.[5]

Is there *anything* that can separate us from Heavenly Father's great love? Consider prayerfully the apostle Paul's response to this question.

"Who [or what] shall separate us from the love of Christ? Shall trouble or hardship or persecution or famine or nakedness or danger or sword?

[When these things happen, does that mean that Heavenly Father doesn't love us?]

No [no way!], in all these things we are more than conquerors through him who loved us.

For I am convinced that neither death nor life, neither angels nor demons, neither the present nor the future, nor any powers, neither height nor depth, nor anything else in all creation, will be able to separate us from the *love of God* that is in Christ Jesus our Lord" (Romans 8:35, 37–39, NIV, bracketed and italics mine).

Heavenly Father's love for you is eternal—it *never* stops.

Heavenly Father's love for you is unchangeable—it is not affected by circumstances.

Heavenly Father's love for you gives—without requiring a return.

Heavenly Father's love for you cares—enough to provide helpful discipline.

Heavenly Father's love for you respects individual freedom—it leaves room for questions, growth, learning, even rejection.

Heavenly Father's love for you is not dependent upon your behavior—He loves you anyway.

Heavenly Father's love for you is totally unconditional—there are no conditions attached. Period.

Notes

1. See John 13:38, NIV.
2. See John 8:10–11.
3. See 1 Kings 3:14; 14:8.
4. Lyricist and composer unknown.
5. See 1 John 2:3–10; 3:9–14; 4:7–11; 5:3–4.

Thomas said to him, "Lord, we don't know where you are going, so how can we know the way?"

Jesus answered, "I am the way and the truth and the life. No one comes to the Father except through me. If you really knew me, you would know my Father as well. From now on, you do know him and have seen him."

Philip said, "Lord, show us the Father and that will be enough for us."

Jesus answered: "Don't you know me, Philip, even after I have been among you such a long time? Anyone who has seen me has seen the Father. How can you say, 'Show us the Father'? Don't you believe that I am in the Father, and that the Father is in me? The words I say to you are not just my own. Rather, it is the Father, living in me, who is doing his work. Believe me when I say that I am in the Father and the Father is in me; or at least believe on the evidence of the miracles themselves."

John 14:5–11, NIV

THIRTEEN

The Acorn and the Oak

The acorn doesn't fall far from the oak tree.

You've heard this old proverb and you probably know what it means. But it's worth another look.

An acorn contains the seed of an oak tree. When that seed develops, it's not going to become a maple tree or a birch tree. Obviously, it will be an oak tree that closely resembles its parent.

So it is with you. When you were a child, adults probably told you something like, "You certainly look like your mother," or, "You sure have your father's disposition." Maybe it was, "You have your mother's eyes," or, "Your ears are just like your father's." These comments might have made you angry or happy, depending upon the circumstance.

As you've matured, perhaps you have observed in yourself traits that remind you of your parents. Whether you like it or not, you have characteristics of your mother and father. Because the acorn doesn't fall far from the oak tree.

This proverb has important implications for our profile of Heavenly Father. It's not a perfect comparison because Jesus Christ is the I AM.[1] He was never created. He has always existed. He is God.

But one very important task He did while on earth was to provide us with a perfect view of Heavenly Father. "The Son is the radiance of God's glory and the exact representation of his being" (Hebrews 1:3, NIV).

Hundreds of years before Jesus came, Isaiah had prophesied that a virgin would give birth to the Messiah and that He would be called Immanuel.[2] This passage was quoted to Joseph by an angel after he discovered that his virgin wife-to-be was pregnant. The New Testament record adds that Immanuel means "God with us" (Matthew 1:23, NIV). So before Jesus was even born, Heaven attempted to tell people that Jesus was coming to reveal Heavenly Father to us.

But people were slow to understand this message. Even Jesus' closest followers had difficulty comprehending it. After communicating with Jesus daily and observing His actions for three years, Philip still pleaded, "Lord, show us the Father" (John 14:8, NIV).

Jesus chided, "Don't you know me, Philip, even after I have been among you such a long time?"

And then Jesus uttered these extremely significant words. "Anyone who has seen me has seen the Father" (John 14:9, NIV). Perhaps the disciples failed to understand this because of their preconceived ideas of Heavenly Father.

Many of us have the disciples' problem. Our misconceptions have made it difficult to obtain an accurate view of Heavenly Father. Yet all we have to do is look at His Son—Jesus Christ.

The acorn doesn't fall very far from the oak tree.

Sometimes Christians view the God of the Old Testament as the Father and the God of the New Testament as the Son. And Father and Son are seen as having extremely different personalities. This may be an oversimplification, but the tendency to view Scripture from this perspective is widespread.

In reality, Heavenly Father is found throughout the Scriptures. There are more than 260 references to the Father in the New Testament alone.[3]

You may remember some of them. Following Jesus' baptism in the Jordan River, the voice from heaven said, "This is my Son, whom I love; with him I am well pleased" (Matthew 3:17, NIV).

Later in His ministry, Jesus climbed a mountain with Peter, James, and John. Scripture records that Jesus' face "shone like the sun" and that He talked with Moses and Elijah. Then a voice from a bright cloud said, "This is my Son, whom I love; with him I am well pleased. Listen to him!" (Matthew 17:5, NIV).

Just as the Father was active in New Testament times, the Son was active during Old Testament events. In fact, He was intimately involved as far back as the creation of the earth.[4]

Not only is the Son Creator, but He has been the sustainer of life. "The Son is the radiance of God's glory . . . sustaining all things by his powerful word" (Hebrews 1:3, NIV).

When the children of Israel left slavery in Egypt and headed to the promised land, they followed a cloud. And "they drank from the spiritual rock that accompanied them, and that rock was Christ" (1 Corinthians 10:4, NIV).

There is little doubt but that Father and Son (and Holy Spirit) collaborated in both Old and New Testament times.

Even the *names* of God the Father and God the Son demonstrate their alikeness. Isaiah, often called the gospel prophet, used many names for the promised Messiah. If you've ever heard Handel's *Messiah*, you're familiar with these names.

"For unto us a child is born, unto us a son is given . . . and his name shall be called Wonderful, Counselor, The mighty God, The everlasting Father, The Prince of Peace" (Isaiah 9:6, KJV).

Jesus, the Son of God, is called "The mighty God." And He's called "The everlasting Father"! So close is the relationship between Father and Son that they share the same names.

No wonder Jesus could say, "I and the Father are one" (John 10:30, NIV). No wonder Jesus implored, "Believe me when I say that I am in the Father and the Father is in me" (John 14:11, NIV).

Perhaps you noticed in previous chapters that I have occasionally applied descriptions of Jesus to Heavenly Father. If you didn't already understand, now you know why that is not only possible, but helpful in profiling Heavenly Father.

My friend, if you ever lose sight of the kind of Heavenly Father you have, look at Jesus.

If you tend to see Heavenly Father as perfectionistic, observe Jesus' compassionate treatment of the woman caught in adultery, who was threatened with death by the Pharisees.[5]

If you slip back into seeing Heavenly Father as angry and abusive, visualize Jesus' healing the ten lepers, whom everyone else despised.[6]

If you sometimes imagine that Heavenly Father is too busy for you or emotionally uninvolved, picture Jesus making time to hold the children on His knee.[7]

If your "early tracings" push you toward picturing Heavenly Father as harsh and judgmental, visualize Jesus' kindness toward the Samaritan woman who had been married five times and currently was living with her boyfriend.[8]

If your early perceptions cause you to feel condemned by Heavenly Father, remember Jesus' words, "For God did not send his Son into the world to condemn the world, but to save the world through him" (John 3:17, NIV).

When tragedy strikes and you find yourself blaming Heavenly Father, visualize Jesus interrupting a funeral procession by raising a young man to life.[9]

When you're tempted to think that Heavenly Father isn't answering your prayers, picture Jesus' response to the request of Mary and Martha to heal Lazarus.[10]

When you question Heavenly Father's commitment to you, look at Jesus. He demonstrated in person exactly what Heavenly Father is like.

The acorn doesn't fall far from the oak tree.[11]

Notes

1. See John 8:58.
2. See Isaiah 7:14.
3. Maureen Rank, *Dealing With the Dad of Your Past* (Minneapolis: Bethany House Publishers, 1990), p. 150.
4. See John 1:1–3, 14; Hebrews 1:8–10; Colossians 1:14–17.
5. See John 8:3–11.
6. See Luke 17:11–19.
7. See Mark 10:13–16.
8. See John 4:4–42.
9. See Luke 7:11–16.
10. See John 11:1–44.
11. See *The Visual Bible*, a word-for-word videotape of the NIV text of the Gospel According to Matthew. It shows Jesus wrapping profound truth and infinite love inside a humorous story, a warm hug, and an understanding glance. In doing so, He gives a clear view of Heavenly Father. Distributed by Review and Herald Publishing.

Once when some mothers were bringing their children to Jesus to bless them, the disciples shooed them away, telling them not to bother him. But when Jesus saw what was happening he was very much displeased with his disciples and said to them, "Let the children come to me, for the Kingdom of God belongs to such as they. Don't send them away! I tell you as seriously as I know how that anyone who refuses to come to God as a little child will never be allowed into his Kingdom." Then he took the children into his arms and placed his hands on their heads and he blessed them.

Mark 10:13–16, TLB

FOURTEEN

Sitting on Daddy's Lap

This chapter is different. Perhaps unique. You probably haven't read anything quite like it.

You will need to slow down, take your time, and use *all* your creative energy. If you simply read through this chapter as a person normally reads, you will miss most of the potential blessing. So if you currently have distractions around you, or if your mind is tired, consider putting the book down for now. (Strange request from an author, don't you think?) But please come back—return to this chapter when you can concentrate fully.

I wish I could be sitting directly across from you. It would make this spiritual exercise easier for you. But there are two other methods of getting the most out of what follows.

You could ask a friend to read the rest of the chapter aloud while you close your eyes in meditation. Your friend will need to read slowly, giving plenty of time for you to reflect.

Or, if you are alone, you can read a paragraph and then pause, close your eyes, and contemplate. Once again, read *very slowly*. Ponder. Enjoy the presence of Jesus. Remember His words, "If you have seen me, you have seen the Father."

Are you ready? Sit back and relax. Take several deep breaths. Just let yourself relax. If a noise should interrupt your meditation, just refocus, concentrating afresh. If your mind should wander or go to sleep, gently bring it back to the scene I am describing.

In your sanctified imagination let's go to a scene described in the Gospels.[1] Try very hard to put *yourself* in the picture. Try to experience not only the sights, but the sounds, the touches, the smells, and the tastes. In an attitude of prayer, picture yourself . . .

On a hillside near the Sea of Galilee. It's a warm day. In the distance sailboats bob on the glimmering water. Overhead, puffy white clouds float through the bright blue sky. Listen to the leaves trembling. Feel the warmth of the sun and the gentle breeze on your face. Smell the scent of fresh blossoms.

The singing of a bird catches your ear. And then the muffled sound of human beings shuffling around and talking softly.

As you focus your eyes on the scene immediately before you, you see people everywhere. Some are sitting. Some are standing. Your eyes now rest on a man you instantly recognize. It seems like you've seen Him somewhere before. It's Jesus!

Jesus is teaching the people who are crowding around Him. Over there are some Pharisees in their gorgeous robes of red and blue and purple. And standing right near Jesus in their plain peasant dress are the disciples.

As you observe, you notice some women coming—timidly—with their children. What do you feel as you see the disciples intercept them and tell them not to bother Jesus? Look at the faces of those women—and children. What do you see?

Suddenly your attention is drawn back to Jesus. He has noticed. And is displeased. He calls the children back to Him. Some run quickly to Him. Others hold back timidly.

Focus on what Jesus does now. He picks some children up in His arms. He sets them on His lap. He hugs them. See their faces light up as they relax in the warmth of His presence.

Now, for a few moments—in your imagination—*become* one of those children. You are no longer a bystander. You are not observing the children. Now you *are* one of the children. Now you are sitting on Jesus' lap, looking through the eyes of that little girl, of that small boy, up into the face of Jesus. You are *so* close to Him. See His smile lines—the sparkle in His eyes. The expression on His face tells you that He's enjoying your presence. You sense kindness, compassion, and love.

You become aware of His strong arm around you. His touch is so reassuring. His strength so calming. You hear a gentle masculine voice say *your* name. You feel His chest vibrate as He speaks. You have never heard your name expressed just that way. It sounds so wonderful and you feel so good. You are smiling from the inside out.

And Jesus begins telling *you* a story. You attentively observe His face as He speaks: "There once was a very good shepherd who loved his sheep very much. He took good care of them. Every day he led them to green grass, cool shade, and clear water. But one night when he led his sheep back to their shelter and he counted them carefully one by one, there were only ninety-nine. One sheep was missing. One lamb was lost somewhere in the dangerous darkness. So the good shepherd went out into the dark, cold night looking for his lost lamb. Finally, after searching all night, he found the lamb and carried it back to the shelter."[2]

As Jesus finishes His story, He looks deep into *your* eyes and says, "Do you know what? I am the good shepherd in the story. And do you know what else? You were that one lost lamb. I came to find you. I love you so much!"

You sense Jesus concluding His story.

"I wish I could hold you like this forever. And in a way, I can. You see, my Father loves you just as much as I do. Since I will not always be with you physically, He will send you my brother—Comforter. He will hold you. He will help you. He will remind you of our great love for you. I wish it could be me who holds you. But I have to be away for a while. I'll be back soon, though, and we can sit and talk like this again."

You notice that Jesus is silent now. You are filled with emotion and feel yourself responding to His great love. How do you respond? Through words? Tears? Hugs? Pause for a moment now and visualize yourself responding in your own way.

Perhaps now you could say your "goodbyes" and start coming back to wherever you are reading these pages. Unfortunately, for the moment, your time on Jesus' lap is over.

Did you notice God's hugs in the story? They're there. Did you feel Heavenly Father's hugs as you pictured the scene? I certainly hope so (if you didn't, try experiencing this chapter on another occasion).

Treasure this special time you've spent with Jesus. Hang on to His promise. "I will pray the Father, and he shall give you another Comforter, that he may abide with you for ever. . . . I will *not leave you* comfortless [as orphans]" (John 14:16, 18, KJV, NIV, italics mine).

The Comforter is with you now. To hold you. To wrap you in His strong, tender embrace. To express your Heavenly Father's unconditional, all-encompassing love—*for you!*

Notes

1. This story is based on Mark 10:13–16; Matthew 19:13–15; and Luke 18:15–17.
2. This story is based on John 10:11–16; Luke 15:3–7; and Psalm 23.

We know that we are children of God, and that the whole world is under the control of the evil one. We know also that the Son of God has come and has given us understanding, so that we may know him who is true. And we are in him who is true—even in his Son Jesus Christ. He is the true God and eternal life.

1 John 5:19–20, NIV

FIFTEEN

If Heavenly Father Is So Good, Why Am I in So Much Pain?

Carl and Guillermo were a few weeks away from graduation. They attended a Christian boarding high school in upstate New York and already looked forward to college life.

Carl Lombard was a "tall, dark, and handsome" Italian. A gifted athlete, he charmed the young women. During his senior year he felt called to preach the gospel. He began traveling to churches with a male quartet of singing classmates. He planned to take theology in college and become a pastor.

Guillermo Puebla was Cuban. He possessed an infectious laugh, enjoyed coed volleyball, and loved to sing. He had committed his life to Jesus Christ and wanted to be a singing evangelist.

One sunny spring day Guillermo, Carl, and their classmates boarded buses for an eagerly anticipated spring picnic. At the state park they played the traditional fastpitch softball game.

After a picnic lunch students got involved in small group games, talking, and hiking. Many of them walked up the trail to the waterfalls. They enjoyed the beauty of the scene and the roar of the plunging water.

Some students waded into the water at the base of the falls, which felt especially refreshing that hot afternoon.

Suddenly there was a cry for help. Everyone panicked. Students frantically attempted to reach Carl and Guillermo, but the undertow began pulling the rescuers down as well. Within seconds the two young men disappeared.

An agonizing hour passed before a rescue team arrived. All they could do was recover the bodies.

Can you imagine the agony of sisters, girlfriends, roommates, and classmates as they returned to their dormitories and homes?

I can. My eyes still water as I recall these events. Carl and Guillermo were my classmates. I heard their desperate cries. More than thirty years have passed since that fateful picnic, but today I can still feel the helplessness, horror, and pain.

A day after the tragedy, I impulsively left school and started hitchhiking home. I was searching for some comfort. And some answers.

Why God? Why? Why did two of my best friends have to die this way? They were so young. They held so much promise for ministry. How could You let this happen? Where are You anyway?

I was pleased when a car slowed. And even more pleased when the driver turned out to be a minister. (I could tell he was a pastor because his collar was backward.)

In my agony, I poured out my story. The pastor said that he had read about it in the newspaper. If he sensed that I was hurting, he kept it well hidden. He blamed my friends for being where they shouldn't have been.

Unfortunately, he brought no comfort to my aching heart. He offered no answers to my confused mind. He presented no solutions to my bewildered spirit. I was relieved to escape his presence.

The universal "Why?" Undoubtedly you've asked it, too. Perhaps you still struggle with it.

For me this struggle began at age three. I was sitting on my Grandpa's shoulders at the graveside service of my one-year-old brother. My question was, "*Why* are they putting Eddy in the hole?" My solution to the dilemma was, "When the people are gone, I'll come back and dig him up."

Your questions may have been similar. Or maybe you asked, "Why doesn't Daddy love me?", "Why is Mommy yelling at me?", "Why did Daddy leave me?" or, "Why did Grandma die?"

Maybe even now you are questioning, *If Heavenly Father is as good as this profile has portrayed, why am I in so much pain? This world is a mess; why doesn't He fix it? Or better yet, why did He permit things to get so bad in the first place?*

There are some excellent resources already available on the topic of human suffering.[1] But these questions deserve at least a brief look here.

Some Christians proclaim that if you "accept Jesus Christ" your troubles will all be over. This theology is attractive indeed. But it's not true.

Let's be honest. In spite of what some preachers say, becoming a follower of Christ is no guarantee of freedom from pain. Followers of Christ suffer. It's always been so.

Ten of the twelve disciples were executed (all but Judas and John). John the Baptist, Stephen, Paul, Joseph, and Abel suffered intensely.[2]

From where did we get this idea that the Christian life is a walk in the park?[3]

Not from Jesus. He told His followers that we should anticipate suffering. "I have told you these things, so that in me you may have peace. In this world you will have trouble. But take heart! I have overcome the world" (John 16:33, NIV).

Not from Paul. He wrote, "I am greatly encouraged; in all our troubles my joy knows no bounds. For when we came into Macedonia, this body of ours had no rest, but we were harassed at every turn—conflicts on the outside, fears within. But God, who comforts the downcast, comforted us . . ." (2 Corinthians 7:4–6, NIV).[4]

Not from Peter. "Dear friends, do not be surprised at the painful trial you are suffering, as though something strange were happening to you. But rejoice that you participate in the sufferings of Christ, so that you may be overjoyed when his glory is revealed" (1 Peter 4:12–13, NIV).

It's clear that Christians should expect trouble in this world. But these same Scriptures make it equally clear that Heavenly Father will be with us through whatever pain and heartache we encounter.

Why am I telling you this? Expectations. If your expectations are based on a misperception of Heavenly Father, you are courting disillusionment. If you believe that being a Christian shelters you from all human problems, your faith may well collapse at a time of intense pain and distress. You may *feel* rejected and abandoned by Heavenly Father, while He is *in fact* holding you close even as you suffer.

Sometimes we set ourselves up for disillusionment. In our hurry to receive the crown, we attempt to bypass the cross. We try to receive the prize without running the race. We forget that we are on a battleground, not a playground.

How very important it is to have as clear a profile of Heavenly Father as possible.

As you think about Heavenly Father's relationship to your emotional, physical, mental, or spiritual pain, I encourage you to consider the following concepts.

1. *Heavenly Father keeps His own commandments.* By that I mean that He will always love His neighbor—you. He

won't lie, cheat, steal, or murder. He can't, because of who He is. His law describes His character.

If it's wrong for human parents to abuse, torture, or kill their children, it's wrong for Heavenly Father. The devil does these things because he hates Heavenly Father and His children. But Heavenly Father will never perform such evil deeds. Unlike some human lawmakers—both parental and political—this Lawmaker is not above the law.[5]

When human parents abuse and kill their children, we lock them up. And throw away the key. How then could we possibly picture the Model Parent performing such terrible deeds?

2. *We live in a war zone.* "And there was war in heaven. Michael and his angels fought against the dragon, and the dragon and his angels fought back. But he was not strong enough, and they lost their place in heaven. The great dragon was hurled down—that ancient serpent called the devil, or Satan, who leads the whole world astray. He was hurled to the earth, and his angels with him" (Revelation 12:7–9, NIV).

With the sin of Adam and Eve, the center of the battle moved to this earth.[6] Today, Satan continues his savage attempt to destroy Heavenly Father and His children.

"Be self-controlled and alert. Your enemy the devil prowls around like a roaring lion looking for someone to devour" (1 Peter 5:8, NIV).

Heavenly Father will bring this cosmic conflict to a happy conclusion. But He will do so only when He knows it is best for His children. In the meantime, Heavenly Father asks you to "endure hardship . . . like a good *soldier* of Christ Jesus" (2 Timothy 2:3, NIV, italics mine).

3. *Sin and its originator, the devil, are the cause of pain, suffering, disease, "natural" disasters, abusive behavior, and death.*[7]

After Jesus' resurrection He visited His disciples. In

order to prove who He was, He showed them the scars on His hands and side.[8]

Jesus' scars bear eternal witness that sin kills. They demonstrate the absurdity of the idea that Heavenly Father kills. Would Heavenly Father murder His own Son? Of course not! These scars also are evidence of Heavenly Father's loving attempt to rescue His children from the consequences of sin.

Jesus came to demonstrate in human flesh what Heavenly Father is like. Did Jesus cause disasters in nature that harmed His people? On the contrary, He calmed the ferocious waves and rescued His disciples.[9]

Did Jesus kill anyone? No. He raised Lazarus, Jairus' daughter, and the widow's son to life.[10]

Did Jesus strike anyone with blindness? With leprosy? With deafness? Not once. But He often delivered people from these maladies.[11]

Did He abuse small children? Never. But He did scold His disciples for shooing away the little ones.[12] And He also said that we must become like children if we are to enter His kingdom.[13]

Who, then, did Jesus say caused all the misery He worked to relieve? His answer was clear and consistent. Once He met a crippled woman in church. She had been suffering for eighteen years. He asked the religious leaders, "Should not this woman, a daughter of Abraham, *whom Satan has kept bound* for eighteen years, be set free on the Sabbath day from what bound her?" (Luke 13:16, NIV, italics mine).

Satan caused the crippling. Jesus, representing Heavenly Father, brought the healing.[14]

4. *There are natural consequences for certain actions.* Much of the pain we experience in life is due to our own decisions and actions. If I smoke, I likely will get emphysema or lung cancer. If I drink heavily, I may well get cirrhosis of the

liver. If I jump out of an airplane, I will die when I hit the ground.

Heavenly Father did not say, "Love me or I'll break your arm." He did not say, "Obey me or I'll kill you." What He said was, "If you sin, you will die."[15] That's a vital difference that many Christians have missed. And what a difference it makes to our profile of Heavenly Father.

Adam and Eve were cruising along on Eden's newest Boeing 777. Heavenly Father warned them about jumping out of the aircraft. "If you jump, you will die."

The tempter entered the cabin and said, "Your Father isn't telling the truth. He just doesn't want you to have any fun. You won't die!"

So Eve, quickly followed by Adam, jumped. They plunged toward certain death—except that Heavenly Father provided a parachute through His Son. Jesus leaped out of the airplane and in a rapid freefall approached Adam and Eve—and you and me. He handed us His parachute. And fell to His death. He died so we can live.

Heavenly Father told the truth. Death is the consequence of jumping out of a 777.

5. That brings us to another characteristic of Heavenly Father. *God respects our freedom.* We don't have to accept the parachute that He offers. We have the right to choose to fall to our death.

Heavenly Father respects our right to make choices. Even bad ones. He doesn't strong-arm us. He will not force us to be saved against our wishes.[16]

His love persuades. It does not compel.

6. *Heavenly Father disciplines.* As we saw in a previous chapter, He loves His children too much to leave us without *loving* discipline.[17]

His purpose is to teach and to help us become His disciples. His purpose is not to punish us. His discipline will help us, not harm us.

7. This one may be difficult for some of you. *There is not always a reason or purpose for each specific pain.*[18] While it is true that Heavenly Father's discipline is painful at the time, and that we sometimes suffer for Christ (persecution), I would venture to say that most of our suffering is not redemptive in purpose.

Most tragedies occur because sin reigns in the world. And sin has never been fair. It never will be. In part, that's what makes it sin and why it's so hateful to Heavenly Father.

That's why suffering is so hard to take. The seeming meaninglessness of it all. It would be overwhelming if we didn't remember its source (Satan). And the glorious outcome promised by Heavenly Father.

8. *Heavenly Father can sometimes bring something positive out of tragedy.* But we should not interpret that to mean that He caused the tragedy.[19]

For example, Jesus brought salvation to a thief hanging on a cross beside Him. That does not mean that God caused the man to be a thief or caused his crucifixion.

And you've probably heard of Lucifer, "son of the morning." One of the most brilliant angels in God's perfect universe. But Lucifer developed self-centered ideas. Thoughts grew into actions and he spread his discontent and rebellion to other angels, then to Eve and Adam—and you and me.[20]

Tragedy of deadly tragedies. And Heavenly Father certainly did not cause it. But He will ultimately bring at least something good out of this disaster by saving those who choose to be rescued. There's another positive outcome. Never again will there be a rebellion. The entire universe will have seen for themselves the tragic folly of attempting to live apart from their loving Creator and Sustainer. There won't be the slightest inclination to desire life apart from Heavenly Father.[21]

Yes, Heavenly Father is able to bring something good out of many tragedies.

9. *Like all good parents, Heavenly Father suffers when His children suffer.* He has feelings and He empathizes with us.[22] That fact was beautifully demonstrated at the tomb of Lazarus.

And sometimes He does more than weep. He miraculously intervenes—as when He raised Lazarus from death. At other times He does not do so, for reasons not fully open to us. Lazarus lived again, only to die once more. Ultimately, of course, Heavenly Father will intervene for all of us: "He will wipe every tear from their eyes. There will be no more death or mourning or crying or pain, for the old order of things has passed away" (Revelation 21:4, NIV).

10. *Try as we might, sin and its consequences are not totally explainable or understandable.* Scripture uses the phrase "the mystery of iniquity" (2 Thessalonians 2:7, KJV).

There's much I don't yet understand. I have questions about the flood, Uzzah at the ark, Miriam's leprosy, the Egyptian plagues. . . . But that doesn't mean that I should stop trying to learn. It simply means that I can't completely understand.

When my son was a toddler, he often looked up at me and said, "S'plain Daddy, s'plain." Jonathan wanted me to *ex*plain something I was doing or saying. At times I was able to satisfy his curious mind.

But there were other times when I was unable to explain a more complex thought or occurrence. This frustrated Jon. And his father. But there was no way even a very bright two- or three-year-old could fully comprehend the mind of an adult.

Our relationship with Heavenly Father is similar. There are many things we can understand. But there is much more that we cannot comprehend. It is impossible for our finite minds to understand the omniscient mind of God.[23]

How do we respond when we plead, "S'plain Daddy, s'plain," and we can't comprehend Heavenly Father's reply? What do we do when, in response to our agony, Heavenly Father *seems* to be silent?

At these times we must walk by faith and not by sight or understanding.[24]

We must say with Job, *Although I don't fully understand, I will still trust Him.*[25] Like Abraham, we will believe Heavenly Father even when we can't make sense out of life's events.[26]

When our thoughts become confused, it is vital to recall what He has already revealed to us. We must bring to mind His warm embraces of the past. We must remember that He loves us no matter what may be happening to us.[27] When we can't see His hand, we can still trust His heart.

When we have discovered for ourselves the type of Person He is, it will be easier to trust Him with the things we don't understand. When we have accepted His invitation to "Taste and see that the LORD is good" (Psalm 34:8, NIV), we will have our past experience to fall back on.

Sometimes, when events don't make sense to us, when life isn't "fair," Heavenly Father simply says, *Trust me.* And because we know Him, we *will* trust Him.

We have found Him to be trustworthy.

Notes

1. Harold S. Kushner, *When Bad Things Happen to Good People* (New York: Avon Books, 1981). Leith Anderson, *When God Says No* (Minneapolis: Bethany House Publishers, 1996). James Dobson, *When God Doesn't Make Sense* (Wheaton, Ill.: Tyndale House Publishers, Inc., 1993). Philip Yancey, *Where Is God When It Hurts?* (Grand Rapids, Mich.: Zondervan Publishing House, 1977). Richard W. Coffen, *When God Sheds Tears* (Hagerstown, Md.: Review and Herald Publishing Association, 1994).
2. See Hebrews 11.
3. Thanks to Dr. James Dobson for the concepts expressed in this section. See *When God Doesn't Make Sense*, pp. 37–40.
4. See also 2 Timothy 3:12 and 2 Corinthians 1:3–11.
5. See Hebrews 6:17–18; Psalm 19:7; Romans 2:17–27; 7:12–14; 13:8–10; 1 Timothy 1:8; James 2:10.
6. See Genesis 3.
7. See Job 1–2.
8. See John 20:19–20.
9. See Mark 4:35–41.
10. See John 11:38–44; Mark 5:22–43; Luke 7:11–16.
11. See Matthew 4:23–25; 12:15; 14:14; Mark 6:56.
12. See Matthew 19:13–15.
13. See Matthew 18:1–4.
14. Thanks to Richard W. Coffen, *When God Sheds Tears*, pp. 33–34.
15. See Genesis 2:16–17 and Romans 6:23.
16. See Genesis 3:1–24; John 13:10–30; and Romans 1:18–32.
17. See Hebrews 12:6–8.
18. See Ecclesiastes 9:11–12.
19. See Romans 8:28, NIV.

20. See Isaiah 14:12–14; and Ezekiel 28:12–17.
21. See Nahum 1:9.
22. See Genesis 6:6; Psalm 78:40; Judges 10:16; Isaiah 63:9; 54: 7–8; Psalm 34:18.
23. See Isaiah 55:9.
24. See 2 Corinthians 5:7.
25. See Job 13:15.
26. See Romans 4:19–22.
27. See Romans 8:35–39.

I will be a Father to you, and you will be my sons and daughters, says the Lord Almighty.

2 Corinthians 6:18, NIV

Sixteen

Healing Childhood Wounds

Linda grew up in a conservative Christian home. The family regularly attended church services. And in their home the family attempted to implement Christian teachings, as they understood them.

Unfortunately, Linda's mother pictured God as demanding and perfectionistic. In her efforts to please Him, she became much like her image of Heavenly Father.

Linda was a helpful and sensitive child. But no matter how hard she tried, she was never able to obtain her mother's approval. Mom's attitude was, *You could do more. You should be better.*

In her desire for approval and love, Linda became the unofficial family social worker. She attempted to fix problems, manage difficult situations, and mend relationships. She met her own emotional needs by taking care of others.

At age eighteen Linda met an attractive young man. What made Jim especially attractive to Linda was his neediness. He gave her someone else to help. *I know he's not a Christian. Yes, he drinks a bit. But I can work with him to change. He really needs me.*

Linda married into a thoroughly unhealthy relationship. Jim didn't want to be fixed—especially not in the areas Linda wanted to fix. She wanted him to go to church with her. He wanted to watch football and drink beer with his buddies. She wanted him to become a responsible employee. He wanted to stay home and watch TV.

Linda's childhood wounds plagued her adult life. How about you? You may have suffered severe trauma. Or your wounds may have been more subtle. But chances are great that you were wounded. An estimated 95 percent of all families are troubled, unhealthy, or dysfunctional in some way.[1]

For those wounded in childhood, it's difficult to *conceptualize* a truly loving Heavenly Parent. If that intellectual understanding is hard, living an *experiential* relationship with Him is even more difficult. But it's crucial to get both our thoughts and our feelings involved in our relationship with Heavenly Father. I know it's a cliché, but half a relationship *is* like kissing your sister or brother. A peck on the cheek is not emotionally fulfilling.

When I refer to the need for emotion in our relationship with God, I'm not talking about the hysterical frenzy manufactured by a sweating, screaming preacher and a loud band. I'm referring to a deep feeling of being loved and the response of loving in return. This relationship isn't based on emotion. But there's definitely emotion permeating the relationship.

Your early experiences may have taught you to suppress your emotions. Or your pain may have been so intense that it has remained in your subconscious. Now, as an adult, you can't allow yourself to feel your emotions, let alone express them. And if you do, they come out at the wrong time, with the wrong person, or in a messed up way.

Difficulty expressing emotions in healthy ways strains

personal relationships. It also restricts your relationship with Heavenly Father.

Is there any hope? Can your childhood wounds be healed? Can you learn to develop healthy intimate relationships? Can you have positive feelings for Heavenly Father? *Yes. Yes. Yes.* And, *yes.*

The healing can begin now, if it hasn't already started. Your relationships can be changed. Your life can be enjoyable.

But it may be a painful process. And it will take some time. In fact, the work will never be truly completed for any of us—at least until Heavenly Father sends His Son to make all things new. But you need to work at it now—patiently and consistently. It will be worth your effort.

There are many excellent books that deal with healing childhood pain (see the appendix). *The Embrace of God* is not a "how to" book. Perhaps, though, it can serve to give you hope for something better, point you toward available resources, and get you started on your healing journey.

Many psychotherapists have written about stages in the healing process. We'll briefly look at just two of those stages.

First, your pain and its source must be acknowledged and honestly faced. Denial of the problem's existence or repeating trite religious sayings—"just have more faith"—won't solve complex psychological problems. Unfortunately, these methods of escaping reality are well-used by Christians. A person must be willing to be internally honest or there is no hope for healing.

Struggling through this stage in the healing process increases your awareness of Mom and Dad's impact upon you. It will probably arouse more pain and anger. But those emotions were already there—and they need to be dealt with in nonharmful ways. That's why it's so important to have a safe environment with a caring professional.

Many Christians haven't faced their deep feelings from the past. I have sat in Bible study groups where members spent much of the time complaining about their imperfect parents. These complainers weren't teenagers experiencing the difficult process of growing toward independence. They were parents and grandparents! They blamed their lack of spiritual and emotional growth on parents, Sunday school teachers, church school teachers, pastors, neighbors, and friends.

It seems like we haven't learned much from our first parents—Adam and Eve. Remember their response after sinning at the tree of knowledge of good and evil?

Adam blamed Eve.

Eve blamed the serpent.

They all blamed God for not being a good Parent.[2]

It doesn't need to be that way. You don't have to stumble through life angry because your parents were imperfect. Frustrated because they were neglectful. Enraged because they were abusive.

Within the healing process you acknowledge that your parents also had parents. They, too, were probably wounded.

How vital it is that you face your past and deal with the pain and anger! Maybe it's time to stop denying your pain. Possibly it's time to stop blaming others. Perhaps it's time to take responsibility for your own healing.

Another significant stage in the healing process is to experience positive parenting.

It's a paradox. Recovering from childhood wounds is work that you alone can do. But you can't do it alone.[3] If you have been severely wounded, you will need professional help. Help from Heavenly Father. And help from some of your spiritual brothers and sisters.

The best human resource is someone trained to help wounded adult children in their recovery. How do you locate such a person? Probably not in the yellow pages.

Ask around. Ask your pastor, physician, teacher, or friends who they would recommend. You may be surprised how many of them have firsthand knowledge of competent, caring professionals.

In selecting a helpful psychotherapist, you might take the following into consideration.

1. *Check the therapist's credentials and education.* Be certain that they attended a reputable graduate school, are licensed to practice in their state, and are affiliated with an appropriate professional organization. Don't be fooled. In many states, almost anyone can set up an office as a "counselor."

2. *Don't be afraid to ask questions.* It's your life and your money. You can ask questions by telephone or during a personal interview (expect to pay for this time). What are the person's areas of professional expertise? Do they work regularly in the area of adult child recovery? What treatment methods do they utilize? Will they respect your Christian values?

3. *You may be most comfortable with someone who identifies herself or himself as a Christian.* It may be easier to establish a beginning level of trust.

However, some caution is needed. Just because someone is a Christian doesn't mean they are skilled at helping heal childhood wounds. They may be a fine pastor, substance-abuse counselor, general practitioner, or whatever. But they probably won't be able to help heal your deep childhood pain.

Also, just because mental health professionals aren't Christian doesn't mean that they won't be helpful. Many Christians have been helped immensely by caring, competent, nonChristian therapists. Proceed with caution. But proceed.

4. *If, after a few sessions, you don't seem to be developing a therapeutic relationship, don't hesitate to change therapists.* Talk it over with your therapist before leaving. Therapists realize

that they can't help everyone and they likely will not be offended.

But don't quit. There's someone out there who can help you. Keep praying and looking until you find that person.

Another excellent reparenting source are good nurturers in your church. They can't take the place of a qualified therapist, but they can be extremely helpful.

If you are female, be certain your substitute parents are a couple—not a male only. In spite of the best intentions of both parties, boundaries can be crossed and your fragile trust demolished.

Teachers, mentors, pastors, colleagues, friends can all meet some of your reparenting needs. In fact, it's probably better to have several people involved—then the risk of dependency and overattachment is not as great. Caring people can serve as Heavenly Father's representatives in reparenting you.

And this plan is scriptural. "God sets the lonely in families . . ." (Psalm 68:6, NIV).

Of course, Heavenly Father himself is a wonderful nurturer. His reparenting skills are the best.

But if you want a complete and fulfilling relationship with Heavenly Father, you will need to help it happen. Here are some things you can do:

Make time to read His love letter to *you*. Apply Heavenly Father's counsel and promises to yourself. Insert your name in the passage as you read. Picture Him sitting there talking to you.

Look for verses with positive feelings and emotions. Sense Heavenly Father's powerful emotions toward you. Allow yourself to begin to respond.

Let Heavenly Father speak for himself. Consciously steer yourself away from assuming that He is just like your earthly parents. He is not. He is your Heavenly Father.

Take time to talk with Him. It doesn't always have to be

a formal conversation or prayer. After all, good talks with earthly parents shed all pretense. Be real with Him. He created you. He loves you as you are.

Think about the kind of Father He is. Contemplate a Scripture passage about Him as you go through your day. Often a new clearer insight will come. *I never saw Him that way before. I am sure feeling close to Him right now.*

Keep a notebook of your thoughts, insights, feelings, and responses. On days when your life seems to be falling apart, go back and read your notebook and the Scriptures involved.

Join a Bible study group. Read inspirational Christian authors. Use a variety of Scripture versions to gain insight into the meaning of a passage.

Practice His presence. That is, remind yourself throughout the day that you have a caring heavenly Father. And that He is with you right this moment.

Talk to Him.

Listen to Him.

Enjoy His company.

Watch for His hugs.

Once you become aware of God's beautiful fathering, you will experience it everywhere. In Scripture. In prayer. In relationships. In daily living.

If you could comprehend intellectually and experientially how deeply you are loved, you would never again feel alone, unimportant, insignificant, worthless, abandoned.

Never had a parent who hugged you?[4]

Never had a mother who protected you?[5]

Never had a parent who was a good role model?[6]

Never had a father who wiped away your tears?[7]

Never had a parent who had time for you?[8]

Never had a father who didn't abandon you?[9]

Never had a parent who set loving boundaries?[10]

Never had a father who loved you unconditionally?[11]

You do now. *You do now.* "I will be a father to you, and you will be my sons and daughters, says the Lord Almighty" (2 Corinthians 6:18, NIV).

In Heavenly Father, you have the Parent for whom your aching heart has always longed. He can fill the emptiness. He will soothe the pain.

And He would be thrilled to be involved in reparenting you. You are the apple of His eye. That's Scripture talking, not me. Listen.

"For whoever touches you touches the apple of his eye" (Zechariah 2:8, NIV).

If you have childhood wounds, He wants to heal them. He wants to reparent you. But you must give Him the chance.

Notes

1. Charles L. Whitfield, *A Gift to Myself* (Deerfield Beach, Fla.: Health Communications, Inc., 1990), p. 92.
2. See Genesis 3:8–13.
3. Whitfield, p. 8.
4. See Luke 11:20–24.
5. See Matthew 23:37.
6. See Ephesians 5:1–2.
7. See Psalm 56:8.
8. See Matthew 28:20.
9. See Psalm 94:14.
10. See Hebrews 12:7–11.
11. See 1 John 3:1.

I have loved you even as the Father has loved me. Live within my love. When you obey me you are living in my love, just as I obey my Father and live in his love.

I have told you this so that you will be filled with my joy. Yes, your cup of joy will overflow!

I demand that you love each other as much as I love you. And here is how to measure it—the greatest love is shown when a person lays down his life for his friends; and you are my friends if you obey me.

I no longer call you slaves, for a master doesn't confide in his slaves; now you are my friends, proved by the fact that I have told you everything the Father told me.

John 15:9–15, TLB

SEVENTEEN

A Friend When You Really Need One

Air Force Captain Scott O'Grady was thousands of miles from home and safety. If he ever needed a friend, he needed one now.

He had been attempting to help the United Nations enforce a no-fly zone over war-torn northern Bosnia. Suddenly, on Friday, June 2, 1995, the cockpit of his F–16 disintegrated around him. He had been ambushed by a Bosnian Serb SA–6 surface-to-air missile.[1]

Word went to his family that he had been shot down. American forces hadn't seen or heard from Scott. "We never really knew if he was alive," said O'Grady's father.

But he was. As his F–16 blew out of the sky, Scott yanked the ejection lanyard. He rocketed out of the exploding cockpit and pulled the ripcord on his parachute.

It was a clear afternoon as he floated down from 26,000 feet. Too clear. He observed crowds of people watching his descent. Scott knew they weren't the welcoming committee from the Chamber of Commerce.

Within seconds of landing, Scott was in the bush rubbing his face in the dirt and covering his ears with a pair of green gloves. No skin could be visible.

He was none too quick. The area was crawling with Bosnian Serb troops. They were shooting everywhere, hoping to flush him out. At times they walked within three or four feet of him. Scott froze—hugging the ground.

When night came, he crawled stealthily to another position. As days and nights came and went, he consumed his few rations. He squeezed small amounts of water out of his wool socks and ate leaves, grass, and ants.

His survival kit included a small radio. But his efforts to contact U.S. forces failed.

Or so it seemed. After a few days, allied planes began picking up his sporadic transmissions. But they couldn't verify that it was Captain O'Grady.

Six days after being downed, confirmation came that he was alive. Scott had a friend in the air. Captain Thomas Hanford, an F–16 pilot from Scott's fighter wing, made the first direct contact with him. Captain Hanford was overcome by emotion. "It's hard to fly an airplane," he said, "when you have tears rolling down your face."

The information regarding Scott's whereabouts was relayed to Marines aboard the helicopter carrier *Kearsarge*. Immediately they implemented their rescue plan.

At great risk to their lives, the marines went after Scott. When he saw the helicopters, Scott charged out of the bushes and quickly climbed aboard. On the return trip they took groundfire and barely eluded three shoulder-fired SA–7 missiles. One Marine said it was the roughest helicopter ride of his life. But they made it.

Euphoria exploded across America. The handsome, smiling face of Captain O'Grady appeared on every talk show and news magazine cover. Americans were ecstatic. Scott O'Grady was a national hero.

But he didn't want to be a hero. He gave the credit for his survival to God. He said the marines were the heroes.

"For the most part," Scott said, "my face was in the dirt, and I was just praying they wouldn't see me or hear me. I was a scared little bunny rabbit just trying to hide, trying to survive."

Scott certainly appreciated his marine friends. But he also talked about another Friend.

"I prayed to God and asked Him for a lot of things, and He delivered throughout the entire time," he said. "When I prayed for rain, He gave me rain. One time I prayed, 'Lord, let me at least have someone know I'm alive and maybe come rescue me.' And guess what? That night T. O. (fellow F–16 pilot Thomas O. Hanford) came up on the radio."

When you're deep in enemy territory, it's nice to have friends. Human, and especially, Divine friends.

The parallel is obvious, isn't it? If anyone is in enemy territory, it's us. If anyone needs a friend, it's us. We need help.

We know that one day Heavenly Father will send His marines (angels) to rescue us. This mission is waiting to be executed and will be led by His Son.[2]

Meanwhile, we need a friend. Now. Thank God for the survival kit and radio. Or maybe you've never thought of the Scriptures and prayer in those terms. They help us keep in contact with our . . . Well, I'm getting ahead of myself.

In spite of everything we've discovered in previous chapters, you may still have difficulty internalizing such a positive profile of Heavenly Father. To really believe in this Father who waits to wrap you in His embrace. It may take more time and effort to overcome your history—what you've experienced and what you've been taught. But don't stop growing. Be willing to let the Holy Spirit lead you into a deepening relationship with Heavenly Father.

As you grow through your pain, God has another plan. For those of us having difficulty relating to the deeper meanings of the parent-child metaphor, He takes another approach. He wants to remove the possibility of being misunderstood.

So He calls us His "friends."

Incredible, isn't it? The Everlasting Father, the Almighty God of the universe, calls you His personal friend. Talk about friends in high places!

Jesus, representing His Father, stated, "Now *you are my friends*, proved by the fact that I have told you everything the Father told me" (John 15:15, TLB, italics mine).

Now you (Lynn, Herb, Susan, George, or . . .) are my friend.

Impossible, you say. After what I've said and the things I've done, no one wants to be my friend. Especially God!

Recall with me a story about ancient Abraham. A severe famine forced Abraham to move his family to Egypt.[3] As they neared the Nile, Abraham instructed his wife, Sarah, to tell the Egyptians that she was his sister. Sarah was an extremely beautiful woman. Abraham reasoned that the Egyptians would kill him and take her for themselves.

So Abraham and Sarah lied.

Well, they really only half lied. Sarah *was* Abraham's half-sister.[4] But Abraham intended to deceive.

Word of Sarah's great beauty came to Pharaoh and he brought her to his palace. Deception put Sarah in a horrible situation. Abraham was willing to give his wife to Pharaoh in exchange for his life.

But God intervened. When Pharaoh discovered the truth, he gave Abraham a tongue-lashing and kicked him out of the country.

Everyone is entitled to one mistake, right? Abraham, the man of faith,[5] surely must have learned an important lesson.

Apparently not. Some years later, Abraham, Sarah, and their household moved to the Negev region of Palestine.[6] He told the king, "She is my sister." The king took beautiful

Sarah to his palace. Heavenly Father intervened. Sound familiar?

Then there was the time Abraham slept with Hagar, Sarah's maid. It wasn't all Abraham's fault. Sarah actually devised the plan.

Sarah hadn't been able to get pregnant, even though Heavenly Father had promised heirs as numerous as the stars in the heavens. They decided to help God out. But God didn't need that type of help. Abraham messed up again.

When we think of Abraham, we remember him as a man of great faith—which he was. But we have also seen Abraham the liar,

the deceiver,

the adulterer,

the man whose faith sometimes wavered.

And then there's Abraham the friend of God. Wait a minute! How does that fit in?

After everything was said and done, God still called Abraham His friend.

"But you, O Israel, my servant, Jacob, whom I have chosen, you descendants of *Abraham my friend*, I took you from the ends of the earth, from its farthest corners I called you" (Isaiah 41:8–9, NIV, italics mine).[7]

Notice that it wasn't Abraham who claimed God as *his* friend. No name dropping here. It was Heavenly Father who called Abraham *His* friend. In spite of all Abraham's flaws.

What an honor to have Heavenly Father call you His friend. But that's what He called Abraham. And because of the acceptance you have in Christ Jesus, that's what He calls you.

No matter what you've said, or thought, or done, or been, Heavenly Father is your friend.

Jesus clearly demonstrated this truth. The people said of Heavenly Father's Son, "He is a friend of tax collectors and sinners."[8]

I don't work for the IRS. But I certainly am a sinner. How about you?

I'm so glad Jesus showed that Heavenly Father wants to be friends with sinners. If He didn't accept us just as we are,[9] we would be in real trouble. For we are all deep in enemy territory.

Note that it isn't only Jesus who wants to be your friend. He said, "The Father himself loves you because you have loved me and have believed that I came from God" (John 16:27, NIV).

Heavenly Father wants to be your friend. And not just during mountaintop experiences. He wants to be friends when you're discouraged, when you've just blown it, when you feel all alone in the world.

Just as certainly as Heavenly Father called Abraham His friend, He calls you His friend.

He wants a close friendship with you.

And He will never turn away from your friendship. As a reflection of Heavenly Father, Jesus demonstrated that in the Garden of Gethsemane. Judas led the murderous crowd to God's Son. This friend of Jesus, who had spent days and nights with Jesus for three years, became the betrayer. Yet Jesus addressed him as *My friend, My companion.*[10]

At Judas' worst moment Jesus still called him *Friend.*

That's the kind of friend Heavenly Father is. He's always there for you. In the good times and the bad. He is a true friend who loves "at all times."[11] He is a very special friend who "sticks closer than a brother."[12]

You may have had friends hurt you or disappoint you. Maybe it's happened so often that it's hard to let anyone get close.

But *this* Friend is worth getting to know. He is special. He'll never harm you and He'll always be there for you.

Even when you're trapped deep in enemy territory.

Notes

1. Story based on a report by Kevin Fedarko and Mark Thompson in *Time*, "All for One," (June 19, 1995), pp. 20–26.
2. See 1 Thessalonians 4:16–17; Hebrews 10:35–37; Job 19:25; Revelation 1:7; Acts 1:6–11.
3. See Genesis 12:10–20.
4. See Genesis 20:12.
5. See Hebrews 11:8–20.
6. See Genesis 20:1–18.
7. See also 2 Chronicles 20:7 and James 2:23.
8. See Matthew 11:19.
9. See Romans 5:8
10. See Matthew 26:50, TLB.
11. See Proverbs 17:17.
12. See Proverbs 18:24.

Now we see but a poor reflection as in a mirror; then we shall see face to face. Now I know in part; then I shall know fully, even as I am fully known.

1 Corinthians 13:12, NIV

EIGHTEEN

Finishing Touches

The time has come. We must complete our profile of Heavenly Father.

Our canvas is now colorful, attractive, and clear. The profile draws us toward its Model.

With brush in hand we dip into yet another fresh color on the palette of God's Word.

When we set down our brush at the end of this session, the profile will still be incomplete. Tomorrow will bring new insights and we'll pick up our brushes once again.

Nevertheless, we must now put our brush to the canvas and apply today's finishing touches.

Jackie has no self-esteem. People walk over her as though she doesn't exist, but it barely phases her. She agrees. She *is* nobody.

When Jackie was a child, her father repeatedly imposed an appalling verbal ritual. "Who do you think you are?" he would demand. "Nobody," Jackie was forced to respond. No other answer would satisfy her demented father.

This scene was loudly rehearsed again and again for several years. Eventually Jackie lost her self. She truly believed that she was nobody.

Now, as an adult, that's how Jackie acts. And that's how other people see her and treat her. She's a nobody. A cipher. A zero.

But not in Heavenly Father's eyes. She is the apple of His eye.[1] He is interested in the smallest details about Jackie—even the number of hairs on her head.[2] He longs to nurture her.[3]

He sees her as special and wants Jackie to realize her specialness. He also wants her to know that He is not at all like her human father. He loves her for who she is. He treasures relationships and desires a lively kinship with her.

Eighteen-year-old Beth belonged to a fairly normal and healthy family. In fact, observers saw Beth as an ideal daughter. She was on the academic honor roll. She never was in trouble with school officials. She was captain of the cheerleading squad. She had many friends.

Nothing was drastically wrong inside Beth's home either. It was just that Beth seemed to overvalue her privacy. She ignored her parents and three siblings. Attempts at conversation by family members were greeted with a curt one-word mumble.

Beth *was* busy. Besides attending high school, she worked at McDonald's most evenings. Her parents looked forward to those times she would be home. But they were repeatedly disappointed when their cherished daughter immediately retreated to her room and locked the door. Beth would emerge for the evening meal. But she ate little and conversed less. Family members felt increasingly rejected by their daughter and sister.

One evening her father managed to speak with Beth

alone. Through tears of pain, he once again told Beth how much the family loved her and how they were hurt by her continued withdrawal from them.

Beth responded, "What have *I* done? I've never been in trouble. I'm not on drugs, and I don't smoke or drink. I've kept the household rules. I'm not pregnant. I go to church. I've made good grades. All these things I've done for you and Mom, and you're still not satisfied."

A period of silence ensued before her father found words. "Beth, you *have* done many good things. You know I am extremely proud of you and your accomplishments. But I must comment on something you said. If you did all these things for your mother and me, you did them for the wrong reason.

"We did teach you principles for living. But not for *our* benefit—for *yours!* It is you who will benefit from the choices you've made. Not us."

At this point her father poured out his pain. He told Beth that he didn't want merely good behavior. He wanted a relationship. He wanted his daughter to talk, to laugh, to cry, and to share with the family.

Through misty eyes, he concluded, "Beth, we don't want just good behavior. We want *you.*"

This experience has important implications for Christians. Sometimes even sincere Christians shut out Heavenly Father. We get so focused on our own agendas. Oh, we probably behave properly most of the time. We accomplish good things. And we tell ourselves that we are doing all this for Him. But, in reality, we are the ones who benefit from following His guidelines for life.

This is *not* what our great loving Father desires. He wants a living and loving relationship with us. He wants to be truly involved in our daily lives.

Perhaps for you, as with Beth, the story is unfinished. I pray that you will not be satisfied with good behavior or a superficial connection. A meaningful relationship is much more satisfying. Your Heavenly Father is the nicest Person you're ever going to meet!

Let's take a moment to step back and view our profile of Heavenly Father.

He will always have time for you. He is there for you—physically, emotionally, and spiritually. He holds you and hugs you every day. He cries with you and wipes away your tears.

He has never abandoned you. And He never will. He is not vindictive. He is not harmful or abusive. Instead, He is merciful, a defender of the defenseless.

While He is perfect, He is not perfectionistic. He is warm, caring, and interested in everything about you.

But He is not permissive. He cares enough to provide loving discipline as well as guidelines for living.

He's not overcontrolling. He treasures your individuality and your capacity to choose to love or not love. But when you ask Him, He willingly provides the control you need to resist the devil's temptations.

His love is unconditional. He loves you no matter what. And He sent His Son to demonstrate His love for you and me.

On top of all this, He calls us friends. He wants a maturing relationship. He doesn't want to continue relating to us as a father to his baby. He wants us to grow, develop, mature.[4] To the place where He can relate to us as His adult children. As His friends.

Certainly not equals. Nevertheless, friends.

I was almost four years old. My family was attending a ten-day camp meeting in British Columbia. Actually, we arrived several days early because my father was involved in setting up the campgrounds.

After working all day, the ministers usually played games in the evening. One of the favorites was horseshoes. The best player was the camp superintendent who was also Dad's boss.

Normally my father was an average horseshoe pitcher. But this night was special. He was in a groove and could do no wrong.

Someone would throw a ringer and he would knock it off. Or throw another ringer on top of it. He was, as they say in sports, unconscious.

It came down to the championship match. Dad versus the superintendent. The passing years have dimmed the details of the game. But there's one thing I still clearly remember. Dad won.

I had been carefully observing—walking back and forth with the group as they played. A very little boy, totally unnoticed. Until now.

Running as fast as I could toward our cabin, I shouted with all my might "Mommy, Mommy. Nobody can beat my Daddy. *Nobody* can beat my Daddy!"

As we have reviewed our profile of Heavenly Father, once again I feel like shouting, "Nobody can beat my Daddy!" Indeed, no one *can* beat Him. No one can top Him. No one can match Him. That's why He's so special.

He's so powerful that He created the earth and all its inhabitants. That's why we call Him the Mighty God.

Yet He's so loving and gentle that He cares deeply about you and me. That's why we call Him Wonderful.

He's so consistent and enduring that He is always there. That's why we call Him the Everlasting Father.[5]

Yet He's so interested in you and me that we are always on His mind. That's why we call Him *Abba*, Daddy.

Doesn't it make *you* want to sing His praises?

> Heavenly Father, I appreciate you,
> Heavenly Father, I appreciate you;
> I love you, adore you,
> I bow down before you;
> Heavenly Father, I appreciate you.[6]

What a wonderful Parent. Even though it's still incomplete, our profile of Him can't help but be beautiful. The Model is so beautiful.

My encouragement to you, dear friend, is to continue painting His profile. By

reading His Word,
meditating upon His counsel,
talking with Him,
listening to Him,
watching for His hugs, and
speaking about Him.

As your relationship with Him grows, His profile will become a gorgeous full-color portrait.

Have you ever placed a photograph of a special person in your wallet or on your dresser? The photo may have been of a husband or son sent off to war. A daughter away at college. Parents who live hundreds of miles away. A boyfriend or girlfriend working in a distant city. Or maybe a loved one whose eyes have closed in death.

You cherished that photograph. You studied every feature of that beloved face. It brought back special memories. It renewed hope of a future together.

That's how much your developing profile of Heavenly Father can mean to you. Only much more. Because, unseen, He's with you now.

And one of these days it will get even better.

"In the same way, we can see and understand only a little about God now, as if we were peering at his reflection in a poor mirror; but someday we are going to see him in his completeness, face to face. Now all that I know is hazy and blurred, but then I will see everything clearly, just as clearly as God sees into my heart right now" (1 Corinthians 13:12, TLB).

Much better than a profile. Even better than a portrait. Face to face.

What a thrill! To see for the first time the Parent we have learned to know and love and trust.

The Parent who laughed with us,
grieved with us,
played with us,
worked with us.

The Father who went through the tough times with us. The Father who hugged us,
encouraged us,
taught us, and
loved us.

I can't wait! How about you?

Notes

1. See Zechariah 2:8.
2. See Luke 12:7.
3. See Matthew 7:11.
4. See Ephesians 4:14–15.
5. See Isaiah 9:6.
6. Lyricist and composer unknown.

May the Lord direct your hearts into God's love and Christ's perseverance.

2 Thessalonians 3:5, NIV

Discussion and Study Guide

The purpose of this section is to enhance your study of, and relationship with, Heavenly Father. If you are studying alone, you might find it helpful to write out your responses.

If you are a study group leader, please carefully consider the following:

1. Unless you are a mental health professional, don't try to make this a therapy group. Avoid intensive introspection by group members.

2. Keep the main focus of the group on Heavenly Father. Encourage both an intellectual knowledge of Him and an experiential relationship with Him.

3. Encourage group members to read a specified chapter or chapters during the week and write out their responses to the study questions. Participants will then be prepared to share their observations and questions with the study group.

Whether you are studying alone or in a group, my prayers will join yours (I promise!) as you continue to grow in your experience with Heavenly Father. Enjoy!

Introduction
A Fresh Canvas

1. Recall an incident when you came to a conclusion too quickly. How did you feel when you discovered you were wrong?

2. Briefly describe what the word *father* means to you. How does *father* make you feel?

3. In what ways have your thoughts and feelings about *father* affected your relationship with Heavenly Father?

4. Point to ponder: "If God came in human form today, would we be any different than His people 2,000 years ago? Would we recognize Heavenly Father? Is it possible that we, too, have misperceptions regarding the type of person He is?"

Explain your responses.

5. What can we do to keep from maintaining misperceptions of Heavenly Father?

6. Read Matthew 11:25–30 in several versions.

   A. To whom will Heavenly Father reveal His ways? Why do you think He chooses such people? What does this say about the approach we will need as we start sketching our profile of Heavenly Father?

   B. How do you respond to *The Message's* wording, "But I'm not keeping it to myself; I'm ready to go over it line by line with anyone willing to listen"?

7. Complete the following prayer. "Dear Father in heaven, As I take a fresh look at the kind of Person You are, please . . ."

Chapter 1
Early Tracings of Heavenly Father

1. Think back to your childhood and describe your earliest perceptions of Heavenly Father. Can you identify any reasons for developing such perceptions?

2. In what ways has your perception of Heavenly Father changed over the years? What may have caused those changes?

3. Point to ponder: "God certainly gets a lot of bad press." Can you think of specific examples? Why does Heavenly Father get so much "bad press?"

4. Read John 11:17–44. This passage contains the shortest verse in the Scriptures. "Jesus wept." What are some reasons for Jesus' tears? What does that say about Heavenly Father?

5. Why is a study of Heavenly Father painful for some people? Do you think it may bring you some pain? What are the best ways to handle this pain?

6. In what ways does your concept of Heavenly Father affect your everyday life? Your relationships? Your prayers? Your spiritual life?

7. In your own words, define the word *Gospel*. How is the truth about Heavenly Father related to the Gospel?

8. Read Romans 8:14–16 in several versions.
　　A. How do we become convinced that we really are Heavenly Father's children?
　　B. What differences does it make in us when we realize that we really do belong to the family—that we really are His children?

Chapter 2
Never Too Busy for You

1. Discuss some reasons parents get "too busy."

2. Were there times in your childhood when your parents weren't available when you needed them? How did you feel?

3. As a parent, have there been times when you've been "too busy" for your children? How did you feel when you realized what you were doing?

4. Comment on the statement, "On at least one occasion even Joseph and Mary were preoccupied parents." What does this say about Mary and Joseph as parents?

5. Do you think Jesus understands what it means to have imperfect parents? Explain your answer.

6. Read John 16:25–28 in several versions.

A. How do you feel when you read that Jesus doesn't have to persuade Heavenly Father to love you?

B. This passage indicates that Heavenly Father always has, and always will, love you. He loves you right now. And that means that He's not too busy for you. Discuss the implications.

7. Point to ponder: "The relationship between you and your Heavenly Father is unique. It's as though there were not another person on the earth. It's as though there were not another soul in the universe. Because He is who He is, you don't have to share His attention with anyone. You are His special child. That's one of the benefits of having an omnipresent Father."

A. How would comprehending this concept affect the daily life of a Christian?

B. What does this mean to you personally—on both the thinking and feeling levels?

8. Read Matthew 28:20 in several versions. Then repeat together aloud several times what Heavenly Father tells you through His Son. "(Your first name), I am always with you."

Describe what personalizing this promise means to you.

Chapter 3
Glimpses of a Father Who Hugs

1. Read Luke 15:11–32 in several versions. Discuss the father's attitude toward his sons. Did he love one son more than the other? What feelings and thoughts must the father have had as he watched hopefully for his wandering son?

2. Do you remember a time (perhaps even now) when you were starving for affection? What did you do to get this basic need met?

3. Read Psalm 56:8 in The Living Bible. Describe what the concept of Heavenly Father collecting your tears means to you.

4. Point to ponder: "I believe Heavenly Father still enjoys hug-

ging His people. Little hugs. Huge hugs. He enjoys them all. He enjoys hugging you, too."

A. Describe how you feel about the idea of Heavenly Father hugging you.

B. Tell about the last time you felt embraced by Him.

C. Why do some people (even people in the church) push Heavenly Father away and refuse His hugs? (See Matthew 23:37.)

5. Read 1 Peter 5:7 in several versions. Describe the feeling you get from knowing that Heavenly Father is emotionally involved in your life.

6. Do you think Heavenly Father gives us more hugs than we are aware of? In what ways?

7. What can we do to become more aware of Heavenly Father's embraces?

Chapter 4
Hugs, Hugs, and More Hugs

1. Read Matthew 7:9–11 in several versions. Discuss how this passage relates to Heavenly Father's hugs.

2. Point to ponder: "Some of God's most profound hugs are experienced in the simple everyday things of life."

In what ways do Heavenly Father's practical hugs impact your life?

3. Describe some of Heavenly Father's aesthetic hugs you have experienced. What have they added to your life? How can we become more aware of His aesthetic hugs?

4. Explain: "One reason God uses many relational hugs is that many hurts have come through *harmful* relationships."

5. Relate a relational hug that has special meaning for you.

6. Give a word picture of a dramatic hug from the Bible.

7. Describe a dramatic hug that has occurred in your life.

8. Which spiritual hugs mean the most to you?

9. Point to ponder: "Don't always try to tell God just how and when to hug you. In other words, don't try to dictate to Him how He should express His love for you." Discuss.

10. Read 2 Corinthians 5:20 in several versions.
    A. Describe how it feels to hug someone in behalf of Heavenly Father.
    B. Compare being the "hugger" to being the "huggee."

Chapter 5
The Father Who Never Abandons

1. Read Galatians 4:4–7 in several versions.
    A. What does it mean to be an heir of Heavenly Father?
    B. Study carefully Luke 15:11–32 once again. Describe how Jesus' story illuminates the meaning of Galatians 4:4–7. For example:
    Who did the abandoning?
    What was the father's attitude after his son left home?
    When the son would have been happy to return as a slave, what was his father's response?

2. Describe from experience or observation what it's like to grow up with a physically absent parent.

3. Discuss a time in your life when you felt totally alone and abandoned. Did you feel forsaken by Heavenly Father, too? Were you actually abandoned by Him?

4. Read Psalm 27:10 and Hebrews 13:5 in several versions. Apply these passages personally and describe what they mean to you.

5. In what ways have you been guilty of attempting to control Heavenly Father? Why do you think you had the need to control?

6. Point to ponder: "Heavenly Father is too great, too wonderful, and too loving to be controlled or manipulated. To attempt telling Him how He should express His love toward us is not only inappropriate—it is arrogant."
    A. Discuss this concept. What should be our attitude as we

make our desires known to Heavenly Father? (See Matthew 26:38–44.)

B. How does this statement relate to the fact that Heavenly Father is extremely interested in everything you think and feel?

7. Read Romans 8:14–15 in several versions.

A. What does the concept of being Heavenly Father's child twice mean to you? Why is it necessary to be His child twice?

B. How do you feel when you realize that you may call Heavenly Father, "Daddy"?

8. Heavenly Father says, "I will never forget or abandon you" (see Psalm 94:14 and Isaiah 49:15–16). What do these words mean to you? What other assurances in Scripture indicate that He will never leave you?

Chapter 6
The Model of Consistency

1. Explore some ways human parents are inconsistent.
   Why are we inconsistent?

2. This chapter examines two ways Heavenly Father demonstrates His consistency—consistent boundaries and consistent mood. Discuss other ways Heavenly Father is consistent.

3. Comment on the statement, "Parental structure produces a sense of comfort and security for the child."
   How does this apply to our relationship with Heavenly Father?

4. Point to ponder: "Heavenly Father gives all His children limits. (Yes, limits are a gift.)"

A. Do you agree with this statement? Why or why not?

B. What do you think life would be like without consistent limits?

5. What does Heavenly Father's consistency of mood or attitude mean to you? Is He always in the same mood? Or, is His attitude toward His children, sin, our feelings, our thoughts . . . consistent?

6. Point to ponder: "But I believe that if we were blessed with heavenly vision, we would see a crimson cord stretching through every event in our lives."

    A. Do you agree or disagree?

    B. Discuss the "crimson cord."

7. Read James 1:17 in several versions. Discuss the importance of this concept to Christians.

8. As a Christian, what should I do when I can't see consistency in Heavenly Father?

9. Read Psalm 139:17–18 in The Living Bible. Compare other versions. What do these verses say to you?

Chapter 7
Defender of the Defenseless

1. Lloyd says, "Most Christians can readily recognize abuse when it occurs in human families. What we're slower to realize is that we may have a profile of an abusive Heavenly Father."

    A. What do you think he means by this?

    B. What are some ways Christians, perhaps unthinkingly, view Heavenly Father as abusive?

2. Point to ponder: "I wonder. How many Sherrys are there in your world? How many people are there who need someone to demonstrate what Jesus intended to convey when He invited us to call God our Heavenly Father?"

    What is your response?

3. Read Luke 17:11–19. How was Jesus' treatment of this man different than the way society was treating him? In what other ways did Jesus demonstrate that Heavenly Father is not abusive?

4. How should your church respond if it becomes known that a child or spouse is being abused in the home of one of its families? As Christians, to what lengths should we go to protect the innocent?

5. Read Matthew 18:5–6 in several versions. What does this say

about Heavenly Father's love for the defenseless and innocent?

6. If Heavenly Father is not the abuser, who is? (See Romans 6:23 and 1 Peter 5:8.) Why would the real abuser want to shift the blame to Heavenly Father?

7. How would an innocent person feel if he or she was wrongly accused of being an abuse perpetrator? Apply your response to Heavenly Father.

8. In the context of this chapter, how would you describe Heavenly Father? (See Psalm 103.)

Chapter 8
The Nonperfectionistic Perfect Parent

1. What do you think of the chapter title? Are the terms contradictory?

2. Have you had times when you felt that you weren't good enough? Do you see Heavenly Father as impossible to please?

3. Point to ponder: "Many Christians view Heavenly Father as exceedingly difficult to please—demanding, critical, perfectionistic, condemning. They do everything possible to try to please Him. Still, they feel that they don't measure up to His expectations."

    A. Describe the type of Christianity this view produces.

    B. Why would people with this understanding want to be Christians?

4. Read Romans 7:14–25 and John 3:1–21 in several versions. Discuss the implications of these passages for your salvation.

    A. Why can't we be Godlike with the natures we were born with?

    B. What did Jesus say is the solution to the problem of being born sinful? Discuss what this means to you.

5. What differences are there between the devil's condemnation and accusations (Revelation 12:9–10) and the Holy Spirit's reproof of sin (John 16:7–14)?

6. Read John 8:1–11 in several versions.

A. What do *you* think Jesus was writing on the ground?

B. Describe how this woman might have felt when Jesus said, "Neither do I condemn you."

C. Do you think she ever sinned again? If so, what would Jesus' response have been? (See Matthew 18:21–22.)

7. Point to ponder: "What she had been looking for in the street, she found in the heart of Jesus Christ."

Discuss what she was looking for and what she found.

8. Read Romans 8:31–34 in The Living Bible.

A. What reasons are given to show that Heavenly Father and Jesus Christ can't be the condemners? (See also John 3:17.)

B. Can you think of other reasons?

9. Point to ponder: "Who then is the condemner? It is the devil, Satan. Scripture calls him 'the accuser of our brethren.' "

A. Why would Satan want us to feel hopeless?

B. What can we do to keep from being overwhelmed by Satan's accusations?

10. Lloyd said, "This parent is on *your* side." What does this thought mean to you?

Chapter 9
Merciless or Merciful?

1. Describe a time when you have been extremely afraid. Have you ever had similar feelings about Heavenly Father?

2. If a person is afraid of Heavenly Father, what type of father must they picture?

3. Discuss some "Christian" teachings or concepts that would encourage the perception of Heavenly Father as harsh, angry, or vindictive. Be open and honest here.

Pick one such concept and study scriptures that pertain to it.

A. Is this concept correct, totally wrong, or partially wrong?

B. What must be done to get such teachings to harmonize with the truth about Heavenly Father?

C. Should our Christian beliefs formulate our view of Heavenly Father? Or, should our beliefs flow out of our understanding of the character of Heavenly Father?

4. Point to ponder: "Did Heavenly Father get angry with David's behavior? Surely. Because Uriah and Bathsheba were also His children. Heavenly Father hates sin and what it does to His people. He must have been very upset (a 'baptized' word for angry) that Uriah and Bathsheba were treated so cruelly."

    A. Discuss Heavenly Father's anger with David.

    B. What type of things anger Heavenly Father? Why?

5. Point to ponder: "Heavenly Father stated emphatically that David had kept His commandments. There was no mention of David's adultery or murder. Heavenly Father looked at David as though he had never sinned."

    A. Did Heavenly Father simply overlook David's sins? (See 2 Samuel 12:1–14.)

    B. How complete is Heavenly Father's forgiveness? (See Psalm 103:12 and Micah 7:18–19.)

    C. What does this tell you about Heavenly Father?

6. David prayed, "I seek you with all my heart; do not let me stray from your commands" (Psalm 119:10, NIV).

    A. What can we learn about David from his prayer?

    B. Discuss the significance of this type of attitude upon a person's relationship with Heavenly Father.

7. Read Isaiah 43:1 in several versions. Insert your name in the text.

    A. Why should we *not* fear Heavenly Father?

    B. How does it feel to have Heavenly Father call you by name?

8. What other evidence can you think of that demonstrates that Heavenly Father is not the mean-spirited Person He has been made out to be?

9. If Heavenly Father is not angry and harsh, how would you describe Him? What kind of Person is He?

Chapter 10
He Cares Enough to Discipline

1. Point to ponder: Heavenly Father "is a loving Parent, not an overindulgent Parent. He loves too much to give His children everything they want." Explain your thoughts about this statement.

2. What are the main purposes of discipline?

3. What are some differences between discipline and punishment? Does Heavenly Father discipline or punish?

4. Why does Heavenly Father provide discipline for His children? (See Proverbs 6:23.)

5. Read Proverbs 3:11–12 in several versions. Some people who are enduring a Job-like experience have said, "The Lord sure must love me a lot" (meaning, "The more pain I have, the more He must love me").

    A. How would you respond to such a statement?

    B. Who was it who caused all Job's catastrophes? (See Job 1:6–2:10.)

    C. Would you consider Job's tragedies to be Heavenly Father's discipline?

6. What are some ways you have experienced Heavenly Father's discipline? How can you differentiate between His discipline and Satan's attacks?

7. Read Hebrews 12:7–11 in several versions.

    A. What is the desired outcome of Heavenly Father's discipline?

    B. Consider different purposes for pain (warning, healing, injuring, etc.). Does discipline produce pain? If so, what type of pain?

    C. This passage states that discipline shows that we truly are Heavenly Father's children. Discuss.

8. Point to ponder: "The principles of love and discipline are not contradictory. In fact, love often demands discipline."

A. Do you agree or disagree? Why?

B. Can you think of situations when this concept applies?

C. Can this principle be misapplied? Describe a likely scenario.

9. Point to ponder: Heavenly Father "loves enough to risk being misunderstood."

A. How does this statement relate to Heavenly Father's discipline?

B. What does this say about Heavenly Father?

Chapter 11
The Issue of Parental Control

1. Describe methods people use in attempting to control others. How does it feel to be around a controlling person?

2. Point to ponder: "The church appears to have more than its share of overcontrolling parents."

A. Do you agree or disagree?

B. Give reasons some Christian parents overcontrol their children.

3. The following questions beg for internal honesty. What are some ways you have attempted to control others? In what ways have you attempted to control God?

4. Point to ponder: "Some people see Heavenly Father as overcontrolling and dominating. Have *you* ever wished that He would go away and stop smothering you with His demands?" Discuss your response.

5. Point to ponder: "Heavenly Father has no desire to control His children through threats or any other means. Intimidation may gain behavioral compliance but it destroys relationships" (see 1 John 4:13–19).

A. Discuss the implications of this statement.

B. How does intimidation harm relationships?

6. What are the differences between persuading and coercing?

7. Point to ponder: " 'Be my Valentine, or I'll break your arm.' Is this an accurate profile of Heavenly Father? Does He *demand* love? Does He insist that we do things His way?"

What are your thoughts on this vitally important issue? What biblical evidence supports your view?

8. Read Romans 6:23 and Romans 8:13–14 in several versions. The ultimate control would be physical threat. Discuss who or what kills.

9. What is Heavenly Father's attitude toward His children who reject Him? (See Ezekiel 33:11 and Hosea 11:8.)

10. Read Romans 1:18–32 in several versions.

A. The text says of the wicked that "God gave them up," or, "God gave them over." What does this mean?

B. Does Heavenly Father stop loving His wayward children at this point?

11. In what ways do we need Heavenly Father to control us? How can He control without being overcontrolling?

Chapter 12
Perfect Love, Perfect Father

1. Explain the differences between conditional and unconditional love. Give examples.

2. Discuss the "look" Peter received from Jesus (see Luke 22:61). What must Peter have seen in Jesus' face for him to respond as he did?

3. Lloyd said, "You have received this look." What do you think he means? Can you remember a specific incident when you received that "look"?

4. Point to ponder: Heavenly Father loves us. "Even when we hurt Him. Even when we disappoint Him. Even when we reject Him."

A. What does this truth mean to you?

B. Describe how this concept makes you feel.

5. Read aloud 1 Corinthians 13:4–8, substituting the words *Heavenly Father* for the word *love* or *charity*. Discuss this description of Heavenly Father.

6. Point to ponder: "While His love is guaranteed, our salvation isn't. Our eternity depends on our response."
   In what ways do you agree or disagree with this statement?

7. What are some practical ways we can respond to Heavenly Father's love? (See Mark 12:30.)

8. Based on what you understand about Heavenly Father, define the word *love*.

9. When bad things happen to us, does that mean that Heavenly Father no longer loves us? (See Romans 8:35–39.) If not, what does it mean?

Chapter 13
The Acorn and the Oak

1. Discuss the meaning of the proverb, "The acorn doesn't fall far from the oak tree."

2. What characteristics of your parents do you have? How do you feel about possessing some of their qualities?

3. What type of Person have you perceived the God of the Old Testament to be? Is He a different God than is in the New Testament? What does Jesus say on this subject?

4. What are some names and descriptions that Scripture uses for both Father and Son?

5. Read John 14:5–11 and Hebrews 1:3 in several versions. Discuss the implications contained in these verses for our profile of Heavenly Father.

6. Point to ponder: "If you ever lose sight of the kind of Heavenly Father you have, look at Jesus."
   A. What have you learned about Heavenly Father from observing and listening to Jesus?

B. Why could it be extremely important to keep this concept in mind?

7. Reread the last section of this chapter. Can you think of other situations in life when it would be important to remember the truth about Heavenly Father? Try to match these scenarios with specific words or actions of Jesus.

Chapter 14
Sitting on Daddy's Lap

1. Describe your experience with this chapter. Did you "get into it"? Could you sense Jesus' presence? What did it feel like to be so close to Him? (If your experience wasn't particularly meaningful, I would suggest that you try it again. Be sure you get away from all interruptions and distractions.)

2. What feelings emerged when you saw Jesus call the children back after the disciples had shooed them away?

3. How did it sound when Jesus spoke your name? Describe your feelings.

4. In what ways did you respond to Jesus' affection?

5. Read John 10:11–16; Luke 15:3–7; and Psalm 23.
    A. What do these verses tell us about Heavenly Father?
    B. If you were the only lamb that had strayed, would Heavenly Father and His Son still have rescued you? Give reasons for your answer. How does that make you feel?

6. Describe your feelings as you had to leave Jesus.

7. Read John 14:16–18 in several versions. Discuss how the Comforter can hold you and hug you in the absence of Jesus.

Chapter 15
If Heavenly Father Is So Good, Why Am I in So Much Pain?

1. Describe the first time you wrestled with the universal question, "Why?" What answers did you get to your "Why?"

2. Some preachers proclaim that if you become a Christian all your troubles will disappear. In what ways is this concept true? In what ways is it false? Why is a misunderstanding of this issue so dangerous?

3. Point to ponder: "Sometimes we set ourselves up for disillusionment. In our hurry to receive the crown, we attempt to bypass the cross. We try to receive the prize without running the race. We forget that we are on a battleground, not a playground."
 A. In your opinion, why do we have this tendency?
 B. How can the devil use this tendency to discourage us?
 C. Why is it vital to have an accurate profile of Heavenly Father in the area of pain, suffering, and disappointment?

4. Comment on the statement, "Heavenly Father keeps His own commandments" (see Psalm 19:7 and Romans 2:17–27).

5. What are the implications of living in a war zone? (See Revelation 12:7–9.)

6. Read Luke 13:10–17 in several versions. What does this passage indicate about the cause of suffering?

7. Read again the story of Eden's Boeing 777. Do you see eternal death as a punishment for disobeying Heavenly Father or a consequence of sinning?

8. Discuss the statement, "I would venture to say that most of our suffering is not redemptive in purpose."

9. Point to ponder: "Heavenly Father can sometimes bring something positive out of tragedy. But we should not interpret that to mean that He caused the tragedy."
 Why is this concept important?

10. What is there about Heavenly Father that you can't understand or explain? How do you deal with not understanding?

11. Discuss what it means to you to have an empathic Heavenly Father. How does knowing that He will ultimately intervene affect your daily life? (See Revelation 2:4.)

Chapter 16
Healing Childhood Wounds

1. Why is it important for both our thoughts and feelings to be involved in our relationship with Heavenly Father? Why can it be difficult to have positive feelings toward Heavenly Father?

2. Finish the following sentence: It is important to heal childhood wounds because . . .

3. Point to ponder: "A person must be willing to be internally honest or there is no hope for healing."
   A. Why is this true?
   B. Why is it so difficult for us to be honest with ourselves?
   C. How do we begin to take responsibility for our healing?

4. Explain: "Recovering from childhood wounds is work that you alone can do. But you can't do it alone."

5. Discuss appropriate ways of locating a helpful mental health professional. Does anyone in your study group know of such a person in your area?

6. Discuss the word *reparenting*. Why is reparenting so important? What are the characteristics of a person who provides positive reparenting?

7. Read 2 Corinthians 6:18 in several versions. On a personal basis, what do these words mean to you?

8. Describe Heavenly Father's reparenting.
   A. Share a time when you experienced Heavenly Father's reparenting.
   B. Discuss ways you can assist Heavenly Father as He reparents you. Why is this necessary?
   C. In what ways will you continue to need His reparenting?

Chapter 17
A Friend When You Really Need One

1. Describe a time when you really needed a friend. What were your thoughts and feelings? What was the outcome?

2. Read aloud John 15:15, inserting your name in the text. How does it feel to have Jesus, representing Heavenly Father, call you His friend?

3. Explain how Heavenly Father could call Abraham His friend even after Abraham's lies, deceit, and adultery.

4. Point to ponder: "No matter what you've said, or thought, or done, or been, Heavenly Father is your friend."
    A. How is this possible? (See Matthew 11:19.)
    B. What does this concept mean to you?

5. If it *seems* that our Friend is disappointing us, what are some solutions to the dilemma? (See chapter 15.)

6. What does it say about Heavenly Father when, in the midst of Judas' treachery, Jesus still called him "Friend"? (See Matthew 26:50.)

7. Discuss what is included in a spiritual survival kit. Why are these items so important to the Christian? In what ways do they help maintain contact with our Friend?

Chapter 18
Finishing Touches

1. Discuss how it feels to be the apple of someone's eye. Of Heavenly Father's eye.

2. Point to ponder: Heavenly Father "wants a maturing relationship. He doesn't want to continue relating to us as a father to his baby. He wants us to grow, develop, mature. To the place where He can relate to us as His adult children. As His friends."
    A. Discuss the implications of this statement.
    B. What does this concept mean to you personally?

3. In your opinion, why are relationships so important to Heavenly Father?

4. Describe any deep feelings that have stirred within you as you worked on your profile of Heavenly Father.

5. Paint a word picture of Heavenly Father as you now see Him. Do you see Him any differently than before you began this process? If so, in what ways?

6. Today, right now, how do you respond cognitively and emotionally to your current profile of Heavenly Father? Do you want to sing and shout His praises?

7. What are some practical ways that you can continue developing your profile of Heavenly Father?

8. Read 1 Corinthians 13:12 in The Living Bible. Discuss what this promise means to you personally.

Appendix

A selected list of resources offering help in healing childhood wounds.

From the Christian Perspective

Allender, Dan B. *The Wounded Heart: Hope for Adult Victims of Childhood Sexual Abuse.* Colorado Springs: Navpress, 1990.

Cannon, Carol. *Never Good Enough.* Boise, Ida.: Pacific Press Publishing Association, 1993.

Frank, Jan. *A Door of Hope.* San Bernadino, Calif.: Here's Life Publishers, 1987.

Hancock, Maxine, and Karen Burton Mains. *Child Sexual Abuse: A Hope for Healing.* Wheaton, Ill.: Harold Shaw Publishers, 1987.

Hemfelt, Robert, Frank Minirth, and Paul Meier. *Love Is a Choice: Recovery for Codependent Relationships.* Nashville: Thomas Nelson Publishers, 1989.

Ketterman, Grace. *Verbal Abuse: Healing the Hidden Wound.* Ann Arbor, Mich.: Servant Publications, 1992.

Littauer, Fred and Florence. *Freeing Your Mind From Memories That Bind: How to Heal the Hurts of the Past.* Nashville: Thomas Nelson Publishers, 1988.

Mask, Michael, Julie L. Mask, Jeanne Hensley, and Steven L. Craig. *Family Secrets: How to Restore Trust Within Your Family by Overcoming the Destructive Power of Secrets.* Nashville: Thomas Nelson Publishers, 1995.

Minirth, Frank, Paul Meier, Robert Hemfelt, Sharon Sneed, Don Hawkins. *Love Hunger: Recovering From Food Addiction.* Nashville: Thomas Nelson Publishers, 1990.

O'Connor, Karen. *Restoring Relationships With Your Adult Children.* Nashville: Thomas Nelson Publishers, 1993.

Sell, Charles M. *Unfinished Business: Helping Adult Children Resolve Their Past.* Portland, Ore.: Multnomah, 1989.

Tanner, Vicki, and Lynda Elliott. *My Father's Child: Help and Healing for the Victims of Emotional, Sexual, and Physical Abuse.* Brentwood, Tenn.: Wolgemuth and Hyatt, Publishers, Inc., 1988.

Young, Ed. *From Bad Beginnings to Happy Endings.* Nashville: Thomas Nelson Publishers, 1994.

Wright, H. Norman. *Always Daddy's Girl: Understanding Your Father's Impact On Who You Are.* Ventura, Calif.: Regal Books, 1989.

Other Helpful Resources

Beattie, Melody. *Beyond Codependency.* Minneapolis: Hazelden, 1989.

Beattie, Melody. *Codependent No More: How to Stop Controlling Others and Start Caring for Yourself.* New York: HarperSanFrancisco, 1992, 1987.

Beattie, Melody. *Talk, Trust, and Feel: Keeping Codependency Out of Your Life.* New York: Ballentine Books, 1991.

Black, Claudia. *Repeat After Me.* Denver: Mac Publishing, 1985.

Bloomfield, Harold H., et al., *Making Peace With Your Parents.* New York: Random House, 1983.

Drew, Jane Myers. *Where Were You When I Needed You Dad? A Guide for Healing Your Father Wound.* Newport Beach, Calif.: Tiger Lily Publishing, 1992.

Forward, Susan. *Toxic Parents: Overcoming Their Hurtful Legacy and Reclaiming Your Life.* New York: Bantam Books, 1989.

Lee, John H. *Recovery: Plain and Simple.* Deerfield Beach, Fla.: Health Communications, 1990.

Leonard, Linda Schierse. *The Wounded Woman: Healing the Father-Daughter Relationship.* Boston: Shambhala Press, 1982.

Lerner, Harriet Goldhor. *The Dance of Anger: A Woman's Guide to Changing the Patterns of Intimate Relationships.* New York: Harper & Row, 1985.

Minninger, Joan. *The Father-Daughter Dance.* New York: Putnam, 1992.

Osherson, Samuel. *Finding Our Fathers: How a Man's Life Is Shaped by His Relationship With His Father.* New York: Fawcett Columbine, 1986.

Secunda, Victoria. *Women and Their Fathers.* New York: Delacorte, 1992.

Stoop, David A. *Forgiving Our Parents, Forgiving Ourselves: Healing Adult Children of Dysfunctional Families.* Ann Arbor: Vine Books, 1991.

Wakerman, Elyce. *Father Loss: Daughters Discuss the Man That Got Away.* New York: Doubleday, 1984.

Whitfield, Charles L. *Healing the Child Within.* Deerfield Beach, Fla.: Health Communications, 1987.

Whitfield, Charles L. *A Gift to Myself: A Personal Guide to Healing My Child Within.* Deerfield Beach, Fla.: Health Communications, 1990.

Whitfield, Charles L. *Boundaries and Relationships: Knowing, Protecting, and Enjoying the Self.* Deerfield Beach, Fla.: Health Communications, 1993.

Woititz, Janet Geringer. *Adult Children of Alcoholics.* Boston: G. K. Hall, 1990.

Woititz, Janet Geringer. *The Intimacy Struggle.* Deerfield Beach, Fla.: Health Communications, 1993.